PRAISE FC

Your emotions are a gift from ⬛️ to
threats. They also serve an in ʌny
Christians become overwhelmed, finding ... fus-
ing, either because they misunderstand their emotions, or ꞏꞏꞏ. ꞈem.
When they lose control of their emotions, they feel stunted and fear that
God has abandoned them.

This is why Melvin Hanna's book, *Mood Food*, is a welcome resource
at a time when there is much confusion about the role emotions play in the
lives of Christian believers. The book points us back to Scripture and how
we can use the spiritual discipline of learning to converse with Jesus about
our emotional states and to transform these emotions so they help us discover God's purpose for them.

A valuable resource for group study and discussion.

ARCHIBALD D. HART, PHD, FPPR
SENIOR PROFESSOR OF PSYCHOLOGY AND DEAN EMERITUS
GRADUATE SCHOOL OF PSYCHOLOGY, FULLER THEOLOGICAL SEMINARY,
PASADENA, CALIFORNIA

In an age in which a person's immature emotions can often sabotage his
success and relationships, this is a very welcome and much-needed work.
Melvin Hanna writes out of a wealth of experience teaching students at the
University of the Nations in many countries of the world. He is greatly
respected by students and his university colleagues. This lucid, practical,
and helpful approach to developing emotional maturity is both refreshing
and life changing.

DR. BRUCE THOMPSON, INTERNATIONAL DEAN EMERITUS
COLLEGE OF COUNSELING AND HEALTH CARE
UNIVERSITY OF THE NATIONS

Dr. Melvin Hanna has put his finger directly on an issue behind all mental
health problems and provided a systematic, yet simple, approach. Starting

with creation and how the brain is wired, Hanna shows us how to engage God in our emotions and how this engagement can change our lives. He takes five specific feelings that may cause us either suffering or blessing, provides a clear description of problems associated with these feelings, and gives exercises to correct them. Hanna will take your spiritual and relational maturity to the next level, when you practice bringing God into your emotional life.

E. JAMES WILDER, PhD, INTERNATIONAL SPEAKER AND AUTHOR

Dr. Hanna has set a fascinating task for himself and for us: to think rationally about our emotions. Emotions constitute the driving force behind our decisions and actions. The challenge Dr. Hanna gives us is to harness these emotions and direct them to a constructive purpose.

How do we harness core emotions such as shame, fear, anger, and sadness, to allow them to work *for us* rather than against us? Dr. Hanna confronts this question with the rationality one would expect of a chemistry professor, but with the insight and compassion of a follower of Jesus Christ. God created us with emotions for a purpose: to motivate us to glorify him. The new way of living that this book proposes is the life-long habit of conversing with Jesus about the emotions we feel in given situations and listening to his reply.

As I read this book, I stopped to ponder Hanna's advice. What would my life have been like had I paused to ask God how to deal with emotional situations? The answer came to me before the question was formed. I think it will to all of Dr. Hanna's readers.

I highly recommend this book as an outstanding guide to daily living.

KEITH M. MCDONALD, MD, AUTHOR
A TIME TO MOURN, A TIME TO DANCE, AND
BRISTLECONE MOUNTAIN (OAKTARA)

mood food

mood food

NOURISHING YOUR GOD-GIVEN EMOTIONS

Melvin W. Hanna

Deep River
BOOKS

This book is published in association with The Benchmark Group, Nashville, TN, benchmarkgroup1@aol.com.

DEEP RIVER BOOKS
Sisters, Oregon
www.deepriverbooks.com

ISBN-13: 9781937756802
ISBN-10: 1937756807

Library of Congress: 2013932807

Cover design by Connie Gabbert

DEDICATION

I dedicate this book to the students and staff of Youth With A Mission counseling courses in many countries of the world. Their questions and life stories deepened my own experience and understanding of emotions. Their desire to have written material to continue to mature in their emotional life was the prime motivator for the creation of this book.

ACKNOWLEDGMENTS

This book would never have appeared without the help and encouragement of numerous people. One of the most important is my wife, Sarah. She accompanied me on almost all of my teaching trips where I presented these lectures about emotions. Together, we interacted with individual students and staff attending the lectures. Sarah's observations and experiences were critical in giving the book its present shape and form.

I am grateful to Scott and Sandy Tompkins, who ran the writer's workshop in Kona, Hawaii in April 2011. That workshop, with Janice Roger's teaching about writing nonfiction, helped me to identify the take-away message I wanted to communicate. Thank you, Scott, Sandy, and Janice for your many suggestions that greatly improved my manuscript. Sandy, I also appreciate your encouragement to call Patti Hummel, who I eventually engaged as my agent. Patti worked very hard to find just the right publisher for my manuscript, and she continues to be a source of guidance throughout the publication process.

Dr. Keith McDonald and Anson Garnsey are two members of a Thursday morning coffee group of which I am a part. I am grateful for their willingness to read early drafts of the manuscript and to make comments that kept my book from sounding like a chemistry textbook.

I wish to thank a few of the many people who, over the course of many years, stimulated the ideas that are presented in this book. The late Tom Marshall was the first person to challenge me to investigate my emotions. Dr. E. James Wilder and Dr. Karl Lehman provided insights from modern brain research about how the brain processes emotions. Dr. Archibald Hart has written prolifically about emotional matters, and I am deeply grateful for his input into my thinking.

I appreciate the graphic design work of Katarina Elisabet Hogstrom, who transformed my crude diagrams into figures that beautifully capture the intent of my discussions about shame and anger.

Finally, I wish to thank Kit Tosello and the staff of Deep River Books for guiding a new author through the publication process. Their work to achieve an appealing title and cover design is much appreciated. I am grateful to Adam Blumer, my editor, who painstakingly discovered my grammatical and style blunders and made me aware when a word or concept was not clear. Thank you, Adam, for pointing out my habit of using passive voice. I needed to change that habit to make my writing crisp.

CONTENTS

ONE

EMOTIONS AND THE KINGDOM OF GOD

*The Spirit of the Lord is upon Me, because He anointed Me to preach
the gospel to the poor. He has sent Me to proclaim release to the captives,
and recovery of sight to the blind, to set free those who are oppressed, to
proclaim the favorable year of the Lord.*

LUKE 4:18–19

My wife, Sarah, and I were boarding a train in Nyon, Switzerland,
when it happened. We had just finished teaching about emotions at
a Youth With A Mission (YWAM) course and were looking forward to a
restful two days at a friend's house before returning home to Colorado. The
train arrived, and three friends from YWAM helped us load our seven pieces
of luggage onto the train. We waved good-bye, the doors closed, and I set
about finding a place for all our bags.

Suddenly, a painful realization struck me like a punch in the gut. My
little black tote bag was missing! I frantically searched all around the train
entrance and the luggage rack in the car, but the tote wasn't there. Instantly,
I got a sick feeling in my stomach. In that bag were our train tickets, over
$2,000 in currency, my cell phone, my PDA, our camera, our lunch, and a
bunch of other personal items.

Now my mind raced with anxious questions. Did our friends forget to
put the bag on the train? Impossible. That bag would have been the first
one on. Did someone steal the bag? What would I do when the conductor
came to ask for our tickets? What about all that money? We needed it to
pay our credit card bill for the tickets.

Amid this whirlpool of questions and feelings, thoughts about what I
had been teaching for the last two weeks dropped into my mind. So many
times I had told my students to let big emotions move us to talk about the

issue(s) with Jesus or a trusted friend. So I took my own advice. Sarah and I found a seat, we talked, and I had a conversation with Jesus about the whole situation. My panic began to subside, and Sarah and I were able to process what we would do next. You'll learn the rest of the story later.

This book is about God's design for our emotions and addresses two groups of people. The first group is those who are overwhelmed by their emotions, as I was when the impact of the lost bag hit me. My lost bag, however, was a single event in a life that had been largely peaceful and satisfying. For many people, the struggle with emotions is long lasting and deeply disturbing.

As we have traveled and taught counseling courses around the world, many people have shared memories of their painful emotional struggles. Some involved feelings of deep condemnation. Many of these people have suffered severe physical, sexual, or emotional abuse. These events have left them with the belief that they could never be good enough or measure up to the demands they have felt from their inner selves or from the people around them. In some, this condemnation had turned into self-hatred and self-harm.

We found that other people, both young and old from many cultures, struggled with fears that kept them from entering into the fullness of life or from doing the will of God. Still others wrestled with anger because of the injustice of the abuse they had suffered or because they felt helpless to change an abusive situation. Each of these people had life experiences and emotional consequences that differed, but a common theme ran through them all. These people suffered emotional oppression and found themselves in an emotional prison, from which they felt powerless to escape.

For this group of people I want to raise hope that there is a way out of this emotional prison. The way out does not involve a quick fix; instead, it involves learning a new way of life. In this book I present the case that achieving an ongoing relational connection with Jesus is the first step in a journey out of emotional bondage.

My case begins with a story from Jesus's life (see Luke 4:16–21). Jesus went to Nazareth, where he had grown up, and went to the synagogue on the Sabbath. He stood up to read, and the attendant handed him a scroll from the prophet Isaiah. He read a passage, which in our Bibles is Isaiah

4:18–19. "The Spirit of the Lord is upon Me, because He anointed Me to preach the gospel to the poor. He has sent Me to proclaim release to the captives, and recovery of sight to the blind, to set free those who are oppressed, to proclaim the favorable year of the Lord."

Jesus gave the scroll back to the attendant and sat down. As Luke tells the story, "The eyes of all in the synagogue were fixed on Him." Jesus had their attention. Then he said something that must have startled them all. He said, "Today this Scripture has been fulfilled in your hearing." The people were startled because Jesus, who had grown up in their town, now claimed to be the One who would do all the things this passage talked about.

This story gives us one of the clearest pictures of why Jesus came into the world. He came to release those who are in prison and to set people free from oppression. I believe this mission includes bringing freedom to those whose emotions have imprisoned or oppressed them. Many statements in the Psalms and the Old Testament prophetic books confirm that God hears the cry of the oppressed and responds to it.

On your journey out of emotional bondage, you will discover that God is on your side and that setting people free is high on Jesus's agenda for the establishment of his kingdom.

The second group of people this book addresses is those who have denied or are out of touch with their emotions. I was a member of this group for the first fifty years of my life. My genetic heritage gave me a quiet spirit and a highly developed rational capacity. While growing up, my parents never talked to me about emotions. They successfully hid from me any emotional expressions between the two of them. My father finished only the eighth grade, and his directive to me was, "Whatever you do, get a good education." I followed his counsel and completed my studies for a PhD in chemistry in 1959.

In the culture in which I grew up, the message that cognitive, rational development is more important than emotional development came through strongly. In my travels I have found this message to be present in European countries and, to an increasing extent, present in some Asian countries as well. These cultural messages form a hierarchy in which rationality and cognitive abilities are valued much more than emotional awareness. So, reinforced by family and culture, I learned how to neglect, or not to listen to, my feelings.

During my two years as a postdoctoral research fellow, and after twenty-one years as a professor of chemistry, I found that I could live quite well using only the cognitive processing part of my mind. As I share parts of my story later in this book, you will learn that I always had emotions. I just didn't let them become part of my awareness.

This all began to change one day when, as a student in a YWAM counseling course, I heard a series of lectures about emotions. The lectures introduced me to three powerful ideas that changed the way I related to my emotional life. The first idea is that God has called me to be his image in the surroundings where he has placed me. The second idea is that God has emotions. He is passionate, full of loving-kindness, and angry at injustice. The third idea is that he has created me with emotions and has a purpose for them. As a result of these lectures, I asked God to help me learn how to become a healthy emotional person. God is still answering that prayer.

The first step in God's answer involved learning to become aware of and name various emotions in my life. As emotions came to the surface, I talked to my wife about them. As this learning process continued, God began to reveal to me how my denial of emotions had adversely affected my relationship with Sarah and my three sons. I realized that I had repeated the mistake of my parents; I had not helped my sons get in touch with their emotional lives.

For the next twelve years, Jesus used my life's experiences to continue answering my prayer. Sarah and I served on staff for many YWAM counseling courses. As students in our courses shared their emotional experiences, I found that I had had similar experiences. Now I could become aware of these experiences and give names to many of the emotions I had ignored. Hearing these stories gave me a strong motivation to study emotions and relate what I was learning to what the Scriptures said about them.

The end result of this process was a series of lectures about emotions, which Sarah and I gave in YWAM counseling courses around the world. These lectures and the interactions accompanying them provided more opportunities for discovery of new ideas and applications about how Jesus wants us to interact with our emotions. I discovered that Jesus wants to transform our emotional experiences so we will no longer deny them or be oppressed or imprisoned by them. Instead, a relational connection with Jesus will transform our emotions so they will help us thrive and move us to actions that will promote his kingdom.

The remainder of this book provides a road map about how this process might work for you. The next chapter looks at emotions from a biblical perspective to help us discover God's design for them.

Two

Understanding Our Emotional Makeup: A Biblical Perspective of Emotions

For the flesh sets its desire against the Spirit, and the Spirit against the flesh; for these are in opposition to one another, so that you may not do the things that you please.

GALATIANS 5:17

Those of us who are in touch with our emotions realize they are a powerful and important part of our life experience. For those of us who live in denial of our emotions, something must happen to give us the awareness that we have emotions. When these awareness events occur, we are forced to face the fact that we have emotions and to seek wisdom about what to do with them.

Emotional experiences can be either pleasant or unpleasant. Watching a sunset shimmer on the ocean while waves break on the rocky shore produces feelings of awe or peace. Skiing down a slope that challenges our skills thrills us with excitement. The assault of angry words from a friend, however, produces a bewildering array of feelings: fear, shame, shock, and impotence. Facing a task we don't believe we are capable of doing can lead to anxiety or panic.

Our emotional lives include our desires. We often experience desires that are opposed to one another. Frequently in the evening I experience this kind of conflict. I have one desire to answer an e-mail, but I have another desire to play solitaire on my computer. I'm sure all of us have experienced warring desires. When situations like this occur, decisions are difficult. When we attach values of good or evil to the two sides of the conflict, we call the experience "temptation."

As a result of these life experiences, we have developed mixed thoughts and feelings about our emotions. Sometimes we may wish we didn't even have emotions or desires. In the context of families, we may receive messages that we are not supposed to express feelings. By implication we think we are not even supposed to have them. In the larger cultural sense, many think emotionalism is inferior to rationality; therefore, they do not regard "emotional" people as highly as "rational" people.

Because of this confusion, exploring how emotions are supposed to fit into our lives is important. We will begin our exploration by looking at a metaphor ancient authors introduced, and then we will look at the Bible to see if we can discover God's design for our emotions.

The Rider and the Elephant

We have argued that internal conflicts are a universal experience. In the verse I used as the epigraph for this chapter, the apostle Paul described a conflict Christians experience. Notice in this passage that Paul describes two desires that are opposed to each other. One set of desires comes from the Spirit, and the other comes from the flesh. Many ancient writers commented on this inner conflict and used animal metaphors to describe it.[1]

Buddha, for example, used such a metaphor. He likened our inner struggle to that of a trainer or rider trying to get a wild elephant to do what he or she wanted.[2] For Buddha, the rider was our rational, spiritual selves, while the elephant represented our emotional, desirous selves. Those of us who find ourselves overwhelmed by our emotions will find this metaphor to be very apt. The elephant is so powerful that he can do whatever he wants in spite of all the rider's efforts. Those of us who deny our emotions either pretend the elephant doesn't exist or try to kill it.

A Brief Biblical Worldview of Emotions

We now wish to explore emotions in the Bible. As we do this, we want to keep the rider-and-elephant metaphor in mind. As Christians we need to clarify exactly who or what the rider or elephant is.

I would like to propose a simple way of forming a biblical worldview about any topic of interest. In this book the topic, of course, is emotions. My simplified biblical worldview involves asking questions about emotions from three perspectives. These perspectives and related questions are the following:

1. CREATION. What was God's plan for emotions in creation?
2. FALL. How has our fallenness affected God's plan for emotions?
3. REDEMPTION. What has God done to restore us to his plan for emotions?

The late Tom Marshall, a YWAM teacher, was the first person I encountered who wrote and talked about emotions.[3] His book and lectures gave direction to my own desire to explore my emotional life by answering these three worldview questions. He pointed out that God designed emotions to be powerful motivators of behavior. As such, they would provide the impetus to move us toward a goal.

In English Bible versions we find examples of emotions moving people toward behavior. When Jesus healed the leper, we read in Mark 1:41, "Moved with compassion, Jesus stretched out His hand and touched him, and said to him, 'I am willing; be cleansed.'" When Jesus told the story of the lord of two servants, Matthew 18:34 says, "And his lord, moved with anger, handed him over to the torturers until he should repay all that was owed him." Tom Marshall's idea was that in creation God intended our emotions to move us toward him and motivate us to accomplish the tasks or goals he brings into our lives. He also originally designed our emotions to move us away from evil.

You may recall from Chapter 1 that one of the thoughts that stimulated my prayer about emotions was that God has called me to be his image in the surroundings where he has placed me. Genesis 1:26 is the source of this idea. "Then God said, 'Let Us make man in Our image, according to Our likeness; and let them rule over the fish of the sea and over the birds of the sky and over the cattle and over all the earth, and over every creeping thing that creeps on the earth.'"

Two ideas arise from this Scripture that help us build on Tom Marshall's thoughts about our emotions. The first is that God designed us to reflect his nature and character in the created world where he has placed us. Our emotions were created to move us to be able to do that. The second idea is that God designed us to exercise authority within this created order. He gives us goals that reflect his will for the created order, and he gave us our emotions to empower us to move toward accomplishing those goals.

But our disobedience frustrated God's design for us. This brings us to the second of our worldview questions. When Eve and Adam succumbed to the temptation in the garden of Eden, our emotions were immediately perverted. Instead of attracting Adam and Eve to God, their emotions moved them to hide from God when they heard him walking in the garden (see Genesis 3 for the full story). The result of succumbing to Satan's deception was the breaking of their relational connection with God. Now all the capacities God had given them were focused on themselves. Their emotions no longer moved them to accomplish God's goals. Rather, their emotions now directed them to satisfy themselves.

God originally built circuitry into the emotional capacity of our brains that causes us to experience disgust at the sight of evil. The history of mankind, since that fateful event in the garden, validates the idea that our emotions and desires now attract us to evil rather than make us disgusted with it.

Notice that in the temptation Satan appealed to Eve's emotions, especially her desires—the desire to have pleasant feelings when something tasted good, the desire to enjoy something beautiful, and the desire for the excitement of becoming wise.

So today we discover that our emotions have been cut off from being servants of God's purposes; they have become enslaved to our self-centered desires for pleasure and the power to control others. Our emotions and desires, *cut off from God*, have become part of the warring sides of the inner conflict we talked about at the beginning of this chapter. Our emotions and desires become part of the nature of our "elephant."

If we focus only on the answer to the question of what happened to our emotions in the fall, we might conclude that emotions are too dangerous. Wouldn't it be better if we didn't have them? Modern studies of our brain, however, answer this question and say *no*. These studies show that when the parts of our prefrontal cortex that enable us to access emotions are damaged, something startling happens. People with this kind of brain damage possess reasoning and logical abilities that are as good as ever. When these people go out into the world, one would think they would be able to make decisions with perfect rationality, free from the distractions of emotions.

Unfortunately, this is not the case. In fact, such people cannot make even the simplest decision or set goals for themselves, and their lives fall apart. Researchers came to the conclusion that decision making is impossible without the emotional components of an idea.[4] Another researcher summed up a number of studies by stating, "How we experience the world, relate to others, and find meaning in life are dependent upon how we have come to regulate our emotions."[5] So while it is true that emotions can be dangerous, it is also true that we cannot live well without them. God has made us with the capacity to have emotions. This capacity has the potential of moving us to destructive actions, but it can also move us to make our lives and world a better place.

That brings us to our third question. What has God done in redemption to restore our emotions to their proper function? We find a broad statement of God's activity in redemption in Colossians 1:19–20. "For it was the Father's good pleasure for all the fullness to dwell in Him [Jesus], and through Him to reconcile all things to Himself, having made peace through the blood of His cross; through Him, I say, whether things on earth or things in heaven." I believe our emotions and desires are part of the "all things" God wants to reconcile to himself.

Earlier I described God's intentions for our emotions in creation. Through redemption God wants to restore our ability to manage our emotions so they may once again move us toward him and toward accomplishing the tasks he has given us to do. Our emotional lives also need to be transformed so they move us away from evil rather than attracting us to it.

Now let's return to the metaphor of the rider and the elephant. Who or what is the elephant, and who or what is the rider? The classical view is that the emotional and desirous self is the elephant and that the rational and "spiritual" self is the rider. This view has been helpful for people who do not have a biblical worldview, but Christians need to think through the metaphor more deeply. The biblical view is that the elephant represents the unredeemed person. Such a person is still subject to all the bondage introduced by the fall. This includes all parts of such people—their thoughts, feelings, desires, and "spiritual" aspirations. The rider is the redeemed person, the person who, according to the promise in 2 Corinthians 5:17, has been made into a new creation. Using this definition of the rider and the elephant, we can more closely examine the conflict described in Galatians 5:17, the verse I used at the beginning of this chapter.

Those who have come into a personal relationship with Jesus experience life from two points of view (see, for example, Ephesians 4:22–24). The "old self" lives out of the self-centered nature we inherited from our fallen state. The New Testament refers to the life of this person as living out of the "flesh." The "new self" is born within us when we receive Jesus. This new creature, referred to in 2 Corinthians 5:17, constitutes our "true self." The New Testament refers to the life of this new person as living from the Spirit. The conflict mentioned in Galatians 5:17 is between these two "selves," the one living in the flesh and the other living in the Spirit. The important point is that *both* of these selves have emotions, desires, thoughts, and wills.

In the classical view, where there is not yet a new self, the power of the emotions and desires forms the elephant, and rationality forms the rider. Emotions and desires are more powerful than our rational conclusions, so when we interpret the metaphor this way, it is valid.

In the biblical view, a person who has not yet come into a personal relationship with Jesus has an old nature possessing emotions, desires, and rationality. This person is called the "old self" in Ephesians 4:22. In this old nature, all the capacities God has gifted us with have become distorted and perverted. This old self is the elephant. In the "new self," mentioned in Ephesians 4:24, God is at work by his Spirit to redirect all these capacities toward their original purpose—to image God in the world in which he has placed us. This new self is the rider. The experience of all Christians is that our old selves seem much stronger than our new selves, which came alive when we were born anew. So the rider-and-elephant metaphor is still very apt, but we must apply it correctly. An important point is that we need to train our "old self" elephant so his energy can serve the "new self" we have become through faith in Jesus.

Some Practical Applications of This Worldview

Recently, the study of emotions has become scientifically respectable. These studies have shown that certain types of affective expression are both expressed and recognized in all cultures throughout the world. Though these lists of types of affective expression vary slightly, they include emotions like anger, fear, sadness, joy, and disgust. Modern brain research has confirmed that God created our brains with the capacity to experience a set of fundamental emotions. Two Christian psychologists, Doctors E. James Wilder and Karl Lehman, have proposed that these fundamental emotions are joy, anger, fear, shame, sadness, disgust, and hopeless despair.[6,7]

In this book, I call these fundamental emotions "core emotions." We have the capacity to experience many other emotions, but these other emotions arise by various combinations and extensions of the core emotions. Here's an example we will expand on in Chapter 5 about anger. If we do not process anger properly, it can morph (metamorphose or change) into resentment, bitterness, malice, or contempt. Some writers refer to the core emotions as "primary emotions" and the emotions that arise from them as "secondary emotions."

To proceed with this complex subject, I want to introduce four postulates about core emotions. A postulate is a proposition one accepts as true to explore complex ideas. By applying these postulates, we will see if we can develop a theory about emotions that is in accord with Scripture. These postulates come from our discussion of the biblical worldview questions applied to emotions. They will give us a way to integrate the ideas about emotions into our lives and begin the process of retraining our elephants.

Postulate One

God created our core emotions; therefore, they are his gift to us. This postulate looks at emotions from the perspective of creation.

Postulate Two

Core emotions are amoral—neither good nor bad, right nor wrong.

Remember that both our new and old selves have core emotions.

But, you ask, what about the fact that the fall perverted our emotions? Aren't our emotions involved in the evil we see in the world? Yes, they are, but we need to examine the situation more closely.

Let's begin by looking at God's purpose for emotions. God made our emotions to move us to a goal, to give impetus to our actions. Thus, emotions move us to behavior. We need to look at behavior to answer questions about good and evil, right and wrong. So we can qualify our second postulate by including a third postulate.

Postulate Three

Morality enters in as we allow our emotions to move us to a response. We make a moral judgment of our experience by examining the response our emotions motivated.[8]

Some examples may help. An emotion can move us to make two kinds of responses. First is an outward, physical response; we call this "behavior." My compassion might move me to buy a meal for someone who is hungry. Or my compassion may move me to get involved in a codependent relationship by always trying to rescue someone. My anger may move me to beat or verbally abuse someone. Or my anger may move me to write to the city council to get them to confront an injustice. These are examples of outer responses. Notice in these examples that we may judge one response as evil or wrong, while we may judge the other as good or right.

Emotions can also move us to make inner responses. Here we turn feelings inward. For example, nursing anger can lead to bitterness, hatred, or desire for revenge. This would be an example of a bad response. Emotions turned inward don't always have to be bad, however; sadness, when internalized, can lead to a hunger to receive God's comfort. Anger at injustice can lead to a longing for God to intervene in the world.

Our postulates so far deal with emotions related to their creation and the fall. We now want to consider them from the perspective of redemption.

Postulate Four

The fourth postulate gives us a practical way to bring redemption to our emotional lives. It provides the foundation for how we will approach emotions in the remainder of this book. This postulate is a more complex one that contains four ideas.

1. Jesus is our Great High Priest.
2. He wants us to invite him into our emotions. We can converse with Jesus about these emotions.
3. Through conversations with him, Jesus can transform emotions that in the past have led to destructive consequences.
4. These transformed emotions will lose their power to move us to destructive responses, and God will redirect them in ways that move us toward him to accomplish his goals for our lives.

Let's explore these ideas one at a time.

Jesus, Our Great High Priest, Wants to Be Invited into Our Emotions

Three key passages about Jesus being our High Priest are the following:

"For assuredly He does not give help to angels, but He gives help to the descendent of Abraham. Therefore, He had to be made like His brethren in all things, so that He might become a merciful and faithful high priest in things pertaining to God, to make propitiation for the sins of the people. For since He Himself was tempted in that which He has suffered, He is able to come to the aid of those who are tempted" (Heb. 2:16–18).

"Therefore, since we have a great high priest who has passed through the heavens, Jesus the Son of God, let us hold fast our confession. For we do not have a high priest who cannot sympathize with our weaknesses, but One who has been tempted in all things as we are, yet without sin. Therefore let us draw near with confidence to the throne of grace, so that we may receive mercy and find grace to help in time of need" (Heb. 4:14–16).

"Therefore, brethren, since we have confidence to enter the holy place by the blood of Jesus, by a new and living way which He inaugurated for us through the veil, that is, His flesh, and since we have a great priest over the house of God, let us draw near with a sincere heart in full assurance of faith, having our hearts sprinkled clean from an evil conscience and our bodies washed with pure water" (Heb. 10:19–22).

As you ponder these passages, I would like you to focus on three questions.

1. What do these passages tell us Jesus has done for us?
2. What responses do these verses encourage us to make to him?
3. What are some things that happen when we make these responses?

As you read these passages, I hope you discovered that Jesus as a man was made like us and suffered all the temptations and trials we face. Because of this fact, he can sympathize with our weaknesses. When we are in the midst of a trial, he understands us completely and wants to help us in our time of need.

These passages also talk about how we should respond to him. He wants us to "draw near" to him with confidence and the knowledge that we have been cleansed. He wants to shower us with mercy and grace. These Scriptures provide the foundation for the first two ideas of postulate four.

The idea that Jesus wants to be with us when we are in emotional distress is important. It asks us to move against the programming introduced in our lives because we have grown up in a family and culture shaped by the fall. The fall has also shaped our personal responses to events in our history. What this idea asks us to do is to become aware of our usual responses to our emotions and, instead of making these responses, to *choose to draw near* to Jesus during our time of need. That's whenever we experience an emotional response that disturbs us. Our temptations also involve our emotions or desires. A situation of temptation is also one where we need to learn the new response of drawing near to Jesus.

This postulate is the foundation for our approach to emotions discussed in the rest of this book. As we discuss specific emotions, I will present a model that involves learning to enter into a conversation with Jesus when we are in the midst of each emotion. This model will enable us to recognize and confront some of the practices we have learned from our family or culture. This experiential learning from family or culture has created habits of responding in two ways: either acting out on our emotions without taking the time to process them or denying our emotions and trying to live as if they didn't exist.

Our goal in the chapters that follow is to deprogram these two responses by introducing a new response. That new response is choosing to let our emotions or desires move us to have a conversation with Jesus as our Great High Priest. Through these conversations with Jesus, we can learn how to manage our emotions and desires so they no longer imprison us but instead help us live in accordance with God's design for us. Note that as we learn this discipline, our new person in Christ acts as the rider, and the elephant is trained to serve God's goals for us.[9]

A Scriptural Story Illustrating the Four Postulates about Emotions

I would like you to read the story in Genesis 4:3–7 about what happened when Cain and Abel offered a sacrifice to the Lord. As you read, try to imagine the scene. Cain brought an offering "of the fruit of the ground," but Abel brought "the firstlings of his flock and of their fat portions." The story goes on to say that God regarded Abel's offering but had no regard for Cain's. We don't know exactly how Abel and Cain knew about God's acceptance or lack of acceptance of their offerings. We might use our imaginations and remember that in other places in the Old Testament, God accepted an offering by sending fire from heaven to consume the offering. So we might imagine that fire came down and consumed Abel's offering, but Cain's offering just sat there on the altar.

As long as we are using our imaginations, let's consider this. How do we think Cain felt? We find out in verse 5. "Cain became very angry and his countenance fell." So we find that Cain had a strong emotional reaction to his experience. But in verse 6 we see that God came upon the scene and asked Cain some questions. This picture is a clear example of our fourth postulate. When we have a strong emotional response, God wants to be with us and dialogue with us.

The first thing God did was ask Cain, "Why are you angry?" This is a very important question for us to remember, and we will come back to it later in our discussion about anger. The point is that God wanted Cain to look into his heart to find out what attitudes were there, giving rise to his anger. Anger is only a symptom of something deeper.

But then God went on to make this interesting statement in verse 7. "If you do well, will not your countenance be lifted up? And if you do not do well, sin is crouching at the door; and its desire is for you, but you must master it." Notice that God told Cain that, though he felt very angry, he hadn't sinned yet. This statement confirms postulate two—that core emotions by themselves are not sinful. God told Cain that the result depended on what he did with his anger, whether he would do well or whether he would sin. This truth illustrates postulate three.

So in this one story we find illustrations of postulates two, three, and four. Unfortunately, we know the sad end of the story. Cain did not do well. He kept his anger inside, it turned into hatred, and he lured Abel into the field, where he killed him. So Cain's unprocessed anger eventually resulted in murder. We'll have more to say about this story in Chapter 5.

In the following chapters, we will consider several core emotions, one at a time, and explore how to apply our model to each of them. We will begin with shame.

THREE

FROM SHAME TO A NEW IDENTITY

In You, O Lord, I have taken refuge; let me never be ashamed; in Your righteousness deliver me. Incline Your ear to me, rescue me quickly; be to me a rock of strength, a stronghold to save me.

PSALM 31:1–2

I used to dread the first day of class in a new term. From age five, I have been a person who stutters. Stuttering is always more severe when one has to say his or her name in a new speaking situation.

At the beginning of a new term, the teacher would ask the class to introduce themselves and say something about what they had done during summer vacation. As we progressed around the room, the spotlight would fall on each student. As my turn approached, my anxiety grew into a monstrous feeling of panic in the pit of my stomach.

My turn came. I stood up and, struggling to get a sound out, was finally able to say, "My na-na-na-me is M-M-M-M-elvin…Ha-ha." Then someone in the class giggled. The panic in my stomach was transformed into a kaleidoscope of thoughts and feeling. I remember wishing the floor would open up so I could disappear.

I didn't have a name for what I was feeling then. Now I know this feeling is called shame. Though all of us have experienced this emotion, we often don't know its name.

EXPLORING OUR FEELINGS OF SHAME

Let's explore some possible shame-activating situations.

1. When we are not respected or valued as a person

2. When we have an experience that makes us aware of a characteristic we dislike about ourselves
3. When we are reminded that we are a member of a devalued social group. For example, being a woman in a male-dominated group, an artistically inclined man at a sports-orientated social gathering, or a minority in skin color or religious convictions.
4. When we don't measure up to standards of achievement imposed by family or culture

Let's look at some specific examples of situations you may have experienced. As you remember situations like these, try to recall the feelings you experienced and the thoughts that were going through your mind.

SITUATION 1

You shared what you thought was a good idea with someone, only to have him or her attack your idea, call it stupid, or both.

SITUATION 2

You brought home your report card. It contained all excellent marks except for one course. A family member remarked, "Why didn't you get an excellent mark in that course?"

SITUATION 3

It was recess at school, and teams were being chosen to play games. You were the last one chosen.

SITUATION 4

Your family moved to a different community, and you had to change schools. The students in this school were all included in various groups, but as a newcomer, you were not asked to be a part of one of these groups.

As you think about these situations, list as many feelings as you can remember. Were you feeling angry, fearful, disappointed, lonely? Underlying these feelings was the emotion of shame.

The Origins of Our Shame Experiences

We all had emotional experiences when we were infants that later grew into our shame feelings. God has hardwired infants' brains to connect with their caregivers; therefore, we are born with the capacity to copy the emotional responses of our caregivers. The primary task of caregivers is to help infants have experiences that strengthen the "joy center" of their brains. When infants see delight in their caregivers' eyes and smiles on their faces, they experience joy. Dr. Jim Wilder gives the name "joy camp" to this happiness infants experience when they interact with those who delight in them.[1] Good caregivers and their infants spend a lot of time in "joy camp."

But what happens when infants see something other than delight during interaction with their caregivers? Let's explore a specific example. Suppose a baby messes his diaper. Exploring this new experience, he investigates this fascinating new material with his hand. Mommy enters the room, and the baby is sure she will be delighted to see his new discovery. Instead, Mommy suddenly shows disgust on her face and may express her displeasure in harsh vocal tones. The baby's brain copies the emotions of the caregiver; instantly, he feels disgust rather than joy.

This feeling of disgust, experienced as a response to the identical feeling in the caregiver, forms the beginning of shame feelings. Dr. Karl Lehman believes that at this developmental stage, it is better to call what the baby experiences "misattunement pain."[2] Later when infants develop the capacity to think about their feelings, they associate this feeling with not being what they were supposed to be, with falling short in some way. At this later stage, misattunement pain feelings become shame feelings.

But let's take our example a little further. The good caregiver leads the baby back to joy by cleaning him up. In the process the caregiver lets expressions of delight return to her eyes and demeanor. Notice what has happened here. The parent and infant shared negative feelings, but then they returned to joy together. This process begins a very important developmental task—returning to joy after a shaming experience.

In the course of life we experience many situations that cause misattunement pain, but often the person stimulating that feeling cannot bring us back to "joy camp" like the caregiver did in our example. Our important developmental task of returning to joy after a shaming experience is not reinforced. The result is that this misattunement pain, which later changes into shame, more and more becomes an oppressive force in our lives.

From this example, we can see how shame becomes part of all social interactions. The brain's ability to share emotional states doesn't go away as we grow older. We may lose the awareness of this sharing of emotional states, but when we are in social situations, we may sometimes sense that someone is unhappy with us. Our brains detect this disapproval through nonverbal cues. When this happens, we experience the emotion of shame.

SOME DISTINCTIONS THAT HELP US IDENTIFY SHAME FEELINGS

Feelings of shame are present in many other events in our experience. Making some distinctions to help clarify the content of these events is important. One helpful clarification is to distinguish between shame and guilt.

Guilt has to do with behavior. When we violate a law or standard, whether from God or our culture, we incur guilt. It is an objective reality. A policeman pulls you over on the highway and says, "You were driving eighty miles per hour, and the speed limit here is forty-five miles per hour." You may experience feelings associated with this guilt. If your conscience is active, you may feel an anxious self-reproach. You may feel angry because the policeman is delaying you. You may feel sad because you got caught.

In spite of having these feelings, guilt is an objective reality and is present whether you have feelings or not. It can be tied to specific behavior—

in this case, driving too fast. The policeman can show you his radar device that shows you were going eighty miles an hour. By being guilty, you incur a debt that must be repaid. In the case of violating the speed limit, you must pay a fine or suffer whatever other penalty the judge imposes on you. Paying this debt releases you from guilt.

Shame, on the other hand, is an emotion that comes whenever we experience an attack on our value as a person. This feeling goes along with an awareness that we have not measured up, that we are flawed in some way at the center of our being. Because we haven't learned to name this deeply uncomfortable feeling as shame, we often describe it in terms of belief about our identity. We say the following to ourselves or others:

I feel like a failure.
I feel stupid.
I feel like I can never do anything right.
I feel inadequate.
I feel worthless.

When we examine these statements closely, we see they're not really about feelings at all. They are beliefs about our adequacy as people. Because these beliefs are tightly connected with our feelings of shame, saying, "I feel" is natural for us. The feeling of shame is the fundamental reality that underlies all these statements, so if we were to speak accurately, we would need to say, "I *feel* shame, and that makes me *believe* I am a failure." The problem with shame is that it is about "not being good enough." It is not like guilt; we can not pay a fine to get rid of it. Somehow to deal with shame, we have to change who we are!

ANOTHER DISTINCTION: TWO TYPES OF SHAME

Some authors distinguish between two kinds of shame. John Bradshaw, one important writer in this field, calls these kinds "healthy shame" and "toxic shame."[3] For Bradshaw, healthy shame gives us a sense of being human, of having limitations, of being dependent. On the other hand, toxic shame comes when someone attacks our identity as a person. It comes whenever we experience an event that devalues us.

Louis Smedes, a more recent author, gives us additional insight into these two types of shame by calling them the "shame that we deserve" and the "shame that we don't deserve."[4] We'll give examples of these two types of shame when we discuss the biblical teaching about shame below.

A "Scientific" Definition of Shame

Here I provide a technical definition of shame. This definition doesn't do justice to the power of the feelings of shame, but it helps us talk about and understand how shame functions in our lives. The definition is as follows:

> Shame is what we feel when we have an experience that brings out a lack of congruence between our real and ideal selves.

Let's look at the various parts of this definition more closely. *Congruence* is a mathematical term often used in psychology. In geometry, two triangles are considered congruent when they can be exactly superimposed over each other. Psychologists say someone is "congruent" when that person's outside behavior accurately reflects his or her inner person. So according to our definition of shame, whenever we experience an event that reveals a difference between what we actually are (our real selves) and what we would like to be (our ideal selves), we feel shame.

Now let's take a closer look at the real and ideal self. As we grow up, our families, our culture, and our experiences form in our minds a picture of our ideal selves. This picture may involve our appearance, our skills and abilities, our social standing, our moral capabilities, or our spiritual state. Part of the picture of my ideal self comes from the culture in which I grew up. This culture says that a "really together" person is someone who is articulate, can tell jokes, and is a good conversationalist.

My real self, however, falls short of this ideal whenever I introduce myself to a new group. Remember the story of my experience in the eighth grade at the beginning of this chapter? In that case I couldn't even say my name clearly, but my name is closely tied to my identity. So whenever I stutter as I try to say my name and someone laughs, I experience deep feelings of shame. Those feelings come because I had an experience that revealed a lack of congruence between my real and ideal self.

I designed the next reflection exercise to help you discover ways this definition works out in your life.

> *Reflection Exercise*
>
> Make a list of some qualities that are part of your ideal self. These qualities might have to do with appearance, social standing, sexual identity, abilities, relationships, and so forth. Think back on some of your life experiences and focus on when something happened that made you aware that you didn't measure up to one or more of these qualities. See if you can get in touch with what you were feeling during those situations. Those were feelings of shame. Can you remember what you said to yourself during these situations or when you thought about them afterward? Did the things you said to yourself sound like any of the sentences listed earlier in this chapter?

A BIBLICAL PICTURE OF THE ROOTS OF SHAME

The ultimate root of shame is the fact that we have turned away from God. The first experience of shame came after the fall. In Genesis 2:25, the story of the creation of man closes by saying that Adam and Eve "were both naked and were not ashamed." We understand that statement to mean they could be completely open with each other. They had nothing to hide. But immediately after disobeying God and eating fruit from the forbidden tree, something happened. Genesis 3:7–8 says, "Then the eyes of both of them were opened, and they knew that they were naked; and they sewed fig leaves together and made themselves loin coverings. They heard the sound of the Lord God walking in the garden in the cool of the day, and the man and his wife hid themselves from the presence of the Lord God among the trees of the garden." Because of our disobedience to God, shame entered human history.

Now we can make use of some distinctions we made earlier. Notice that the shame Adam and Eve felt is an example of "healthy shame" or the shame they deserved. They fell short of God's design for them, so the shame was correct. The emotion of shame was there to remind them of this failure. It was shame they deserved because it resulted from their disobedience.

Centuries ago these verses gave the details of our present psychological understanding of shame. The shame experience begins with an opening of the eyes. This is the revelation that we are not what we are supposed to be—that our real selves are incongruent with our ideal selves. God designed us to be in intimate communion with him. Because of Adam and Eve's disobedience, that communion was lost.

Next we discover the two main symptoms of shame. First, shame moves us to hide. Adam and Eve needed to hide from each other, so they made fig leaves. Then they hid from God. People who work with those who struggle with addictions know that the most important component maintaining the addiction is denial.

Denial, an attempt to hide something associated with feelings of shame, is one of the major defense mechanisms first described by Sigmund Freud.[5] All people who stutter feel shame when they stutter. Then they do everything they can to hide their stuttering. The first step that must take place in stuttering therapy is to identify and stop the hiding behaviors.

The second symptom of shame is apparent in the conversation between God and Adam and Eve. When God questioned Adam about what he had done, he blamed Eve and indirectly blamed God by saying, "The woman whom You gave to be with me, she gave me from the tree, and I ate" (v. 12). Then Eve blamed the serpent. Thus, blaming others or being defensive is very often our first response to feelings of shame. This defensiveness can turn into anger. Shame makes us feel small; anger makes us feel big. So often, especially in men, anger becomes a defense mechanism against shame.

Reflection Exercise

We can work backward from symptoms to experiences that have shame feelings tied to them. What are some situations in your life for which you hide or are tempted to hide? What are some subjects you do not wish to talk about? Look at areas of life you avoid. Pick one of these areas and think about it in the presence of the Lord. Do you avoid these areas because you fear the shame feelings they bring? Ask God to reveal to you whether you have some of these areas he wants you to invite him into, so you can begin working on your shame feelings.

Figure 3-1

Notice what God did in response to Adam and Eve's disobedience. In the midst of the emotions that moved them to hide from him, God sought them out and desired to have a conversation with them. This event is another biblical example of postulate four described in the last chapter. God wanted to be with them when they experienced these traumatic emotions. At the end of the conversation, he helped them through the trauma by making skins to cover their nakedness. These ideas are summarized in Figure 3-1.

THE RELATIONSHIP BETWEEN SIN AND OUR SHAME FEELINGS: SHAME AND FALLENNESS

Romans 3:23 says, "For all have sinned and fall short of the glory of God." This verse sums up what our situation is in regard to guilt and shame. Sin is a transgression of God's laws. When we sin, we incur guilt and need forgiveness. Jesus's sacrifice on the cross paid the debt we owe because of our transgressions. So by confession of our sins and faith that God has paid the debt we owe, he can release us from our guilt (see 1 John 1:9).

But we also incur shame because we fail to image God's glory properly. God created us to be his image-bearers on earth. He originally designed us to reflect his glory in our actions and attitudes. God's creation of us to be his image bearers is the foundation for our ideal or true selves. Our sins produce a lack of congruence between our ideal and true selves. We are less than we were created to be, and shame is the messenger that tells us this. So feelings of shame we experience when we fall short of our calling to bear the image of God are appropriate. This is "healthy shame" or the "shame we deserve." These feelings of shame are reminders that we need God to cover our shame.

However, we need to look at the bigger picture of sin and shame. It is not only our sins that bring us shame. Our world has become infected with sin, and people sin against each other. When someone sins against us, that person's actions bring us shame. We see this fact most clearly in the case of physical or sexual abuse. This kind of abuse treats us as objects to be used for someone else's pleasure or need for control, causing deep wounds to our sense of value as people.

But all sins against others bring them shame. We must recognize that when we ridicule or use our words or actions to put someone down, we bring them shame. All of us have experienced the pain of being an object of someone's ridicule either by words or actions. This is "toxic shame" or the "shame we don't deserve."

REDEMPTION AND SHAME

For God to restore us so we can fulfill his original purpose for us, he must deal with not only our sins by forgiveness but also our shame. To deal with our shame, God must make us into new people and give us a new identity. Jesus accomplished both of these goals for us through his suffering and death on the cross. His shed blood becomes the sacrifice that brings the forgiveness of our sins. His taking of our sinful identity onto himself and bearing the shame that results from our sins make an exchange possible. In that exchange he takes our sinful identity with all its shame upon himself and gives us a new identity as children of God. We are clothed in Jesus's right-eousness, and through the power of the Holy Spirit we receive the ability to represent the image of God on earth.

What's important to note is that God is the source of our being, and only God can give us our true identity. This new identity, which comes through our faith in Christ, is described in 2 Corinthians 5:17. "Therefore if anyone is in Christ, he is a new creature; the old things passed away; behold, new things have come." When God brings us into a new relation-ship with him through faith in Jesus, many important steps occur. One, related to our identity, is that he shares his glory with us. Romans 5:2 says, "We exult in hope of the glory of God." Romans 8:18 says, "The sufferings of this present time are not worthy to be compared with the glory that is to be revealed to us." Second Corinthians 3:18 talks about being "transformed into the same image from glory to glory, just as from the Lord, the Spirit." The Bible tells us that we begin to share his glory in our present lives but that we will share it much more fully when we are with him.

What does all this have to do with shame? The opposite of being shamed is being honored. To be invited to share the glory of God is a powerful experience of being honored instead of shamed. So just as Jesus "for the joy set before Him endured the cross, despising the shame" (Heb. 12:2), God gives us power by faith to despise the shame we feel because of our hope of sharing the glory of God.

A second step that happens, related to our identity, is that God accepts us. A core belief that empowers feelings of shame is that we are unacceptable (note how this feeling of being unacceptable links back to the experience of the infant and caregiver). So the beginning of our healing from shame comes from the experience of God's grace when he accepts us.

As we saw earlier, experiences of shame are all about not measuring up. If we don't measure up, the fear of not being accepted (or of being rejected) rises up within us. So to be released from the destructive effects of shame feelings, we must experience God's grace. What are some of the ways we experience this grace? Louis Smedes gives us a powerful summary.[6]

- We experience grace as pardon: we are forgiven for wrongs we have done. Pardoning grace is the answer to guilt.
- We experience grace as acceptance: we are reunited with God and with our true selves, accepted, cradled, held, affirmed, and loved. Accepting grace is the answer to shame.
- We experience grace as power: it provides a spiritual energy to shed the heaviness of shame and move toward the true self God means us to be.
- We experience grace as gratitude: it gives us a sense for the gift of life, a gift of wonder and sometimes elation at the lavish generosity of God.

WORKING WITH OUR SHAME FEELINGS: CONVERSATIONS WITH JESUS, OUR HIGH PRIEST

Shame is a universal experience, and we will never be free from the feelings produced by shaming events until we are with Jesus and fully experience sharing his glory in the new heaven and new earth. In this life, however, we can be released from the oppressive consequences of shame, such as self-hatred, condemnation, withdrawal, hiding, and defensiveness. In this section we trace some steps we can take to battle against these consequences that seek to imprison us. We learn how to train our "elephants" to respond to feelings of shame differently.

To get started, we need to have our eyes opened. We need to learn to recognize shame from its initial effects in our lives. "Having our eyes opened" means that when we experience the temptation to hide or become defensive, we realize that something happens in our lives to stimulate shame. Our task then is to resist this temptation and instead seek insight into the source of our shame feelings.

We need to learn to welcome these shame feelings and let them move us to have a conversation with Jesus. Remember, God looked for Adam and Eve after they had sinned. Likewise, in the form of Jesus, he wants to be present with us when we are in the midst of painful feelings of shame. We can talk to Jesus about how we feel and about what these feelings move us to do.

As we talk with Jesus about being released from destructive consequences of shame, we need to remember the cross and ponder its meaning. Jesus's death on the cross demonstrated God's great love for us. Jesus did everything necessary to undo the effects of the fall and restore us to God's family.

The first thing Jesus accomplished for us was to make the forgiveness of our sins possible. In 1 John 1:7b, 9 we find, "And the blood of Jesus His Son cleanses us from all sin…If we confess our sins, He is faithful and righteous to forgive us our sins and to cleanse us from all unrighteousness." Furthermore, in 2 Corinthians 5:21 we read, "He made Him who knew no sin to be sin on our behalf, so that we might become the righteousness of God in Him."

A second thing Jesus did for us was to bear our shame. Consider the events that occurred in Jesus's life between the garden of Gethsemane and his burial in the tomb. Three of his closest disciples couldn't watch with him as he prayed in agony. They went to sleep. One of his disciples betrayed him to those who wanted to destroy him. When the temple guards came to arrest him, most of his disciples abandoned him. He was unjustly accused, abused, and mocked at his trial. He was again unjustly accused at a public trial before Pontius Pilate. Roman soldiers tortured and mocked him. He was forced to carry a cross through the streets of Jerusalem. Finally, he was hung naked on a cross and further mocked by the Jewish rulers.

What do these events have in common? They produce shame. By suffering in these ways, Jesus carried our shame to the cross. A second powerful message we receive as we consider the cross is that when Jesus was placed in the tomb, our shame, which he had unjustly borne, was buried with him.

Remembering both of these accomplishments as we meditate on the cross reminds us that a twofold exchange took place there. First, Jesus exchanged his righteousness for our sinfulness. Second, he exchanged his identity as the beloved Son of God for our shame-filled identity. As we converse with Jesus when we are in the midst of painful shame feelings, we are reminded of these exchanges. We now have a new identity, which we must receive by faith in the same way we receive the forgiveness of our sins by faith. We receive both as gifts of grace. This new identity means God has accepted us as his sons and daughters in spite of all our shortcomings. The top part of Figure 3-2 depicts this process.

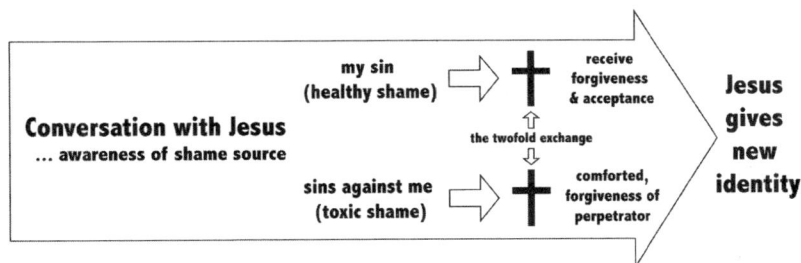

Figure 3-2

As we have this conversation with Jesus, we must remember that shame comes to us as a result of sin, either because of our own sins or because of the sins of others against us. The first part of our conversation seeks insight into the ways our sin has been responsible for our shame feelings. We experience release from this shame we deserve by confessing our sins, receiving his forgiveness, and reaffirming his gift of our new identity.

As our conversation continues, we may discover that we have sinned by replacing God as the center of our life with something less. Let's explore this idea further from Scripture. First, let's look at Jeremiah 2:13. "For my people have committed two evils: they have forsaken Me, the fountain of living waters, to hew for themselves cisterns, broken cisterns that can hold no water." Then we should consider Romans 1:23. "[They] exchanged the glory of the incorruptible God for an image in the form of corruptible man and of birds and four-footed animals and crawling creatures."

These two verses give important insight into what we often do when we have an inadequate sense of identity. Instead of letting God give us our true identity as his sons or daughters, we try to establish our own identity. These efforts to establish our identities are the "broken cisterns" we construct that can "hold no water." They become idols we have adopted to hide our nakedness and incompleteness without God. They are our fig leaves.

What are some of these "broken cisterns"? We try to perform to make ourselves acceptable. We acquire money and wealth to try to be significant. We seek status and power to be somebody. We try to use our appearance or relationships to prove we are okay. As we continue our conversation with Jesus at the cross, we must let him reveal to us any of these things we have used to try to cover our shame rather than receiving our identity from God. These are all symptoms of "exchang[ing] the glory of the incorruptible God" at the center of our being for an "image in the form of corruptible man." If we receive revelation from God that we have tried to establish our own identities in any of these ways, we must confess our sin of idolatry to the Lord and renounce these idols. We then receive Jesus's cleansing and forgiveness, and give our feelings of shame to Jesus to bear for us on the cross.

We now have insight into how our own falling short has influenced our shame, but we need to turn to the second source of shame. This is shame that comes because of sins of others against us. This is "toxic shame" or the "shame we don't deserve." Discovering how to find freedom from the shaming effects of the sins of others against us will also help us when a similar situation arises that requires us to consider anger and sadness. The following ideas may be new, so this process needs some elaboration.

HOW REDEMPTION PROVIDES RELEASE FROM THE SINS OF OTHERS AGAINST US

When Jesus died on the cross, he died not only for our sins but also for the sins of those who have sinned against us. For us to be set free from the effects of sin others have committed against us, we must be able to name the evil that has come to us, bring that evil to Jesus on the cross, and experience Jesus's release for us.

Two steps are necessary to receive this release. The first step is to experience Jesus's comfort for the pain and loss that have come to us as the result of another person's sin. This kind of experience is sometimes called "healing of memories," which we will say more about in the next section. The second necessary step is to receive grace from Jesus to forgive the person who has wounded us. This, too, is a process that takes place as we meditate on what he accomplished for us on the cross.

We learned as we read the passages about Jesus being our High Priest that part of Jesus's acting as our High Priest is that we believe God wants to comfort us in our losses and emotional pain, and give us grace to forgive those who have wounded us. This belief is anchored in the fact that Jesus carried the shame that came through the sins of others against us. We argued above that between Gethsemane and his burial, Jesus experienced every possible shaming event. Because he experienced every possible source of shame, due to the sins of others against him, he can bring understanding and comfort when others have shamefully treated us.

As we offer this kind of shame to Jesus in our conversation, we need a genuine experience of his presence to comfort us. This comfort can come as we pour out our feelings about all the losses we have experienced because of the sins of others against us. This comfort comes as a gift of grace as we are enabled to see the other person as Jesus sees him or her.

Finally, when we follow Jesus's example of praying, "Father, forgive them for they know not what they do," we ask for grace to forgive those who have sinned against us.[7] The bottom part of Figure 3-2 shows this process.

THE ROLE OF FAITH IN LIVING FROM OUR NEW IDENTITY AS CHILDREN OF GOD

The final step to be released from the destructive effects of shame is to receive, by faith, God's acceptance of us and the gift of our new identity in Christ. This includes our identity as God's sons or daughters, as Jesus's friends and brothers, as the bride of Christ, as part of his body reflecting his glory, as a clay pot that contains the glory of God, and as one over whom our Father sings for joy. These are all things the Scriptures say about us.

It is good to hold up our hands as we talk with Jesus and openly receive this gift of God's grace. In order to fully receive it, we need to meditate on New Testament passages that describe this new identity. This ongoing project is described in the next Reflection Exercise, but we can begin with 2 Corinthians 5:17 (cited above) and Romans 6:4. "Therefore we have been buried with Him through baptism into death, so that as Christ was raised from the dead through the glory of the Father, so we too might walk in newness of life."

Reflection Exercise

Many New Testament passages talk about who we are in Christ. Begin a project of making a list of these passages in a journal and then prayerfully meditating on them by personalizing them with your own name or the pronouns *I* or *me*. Use them to help you affirm your new identity in Christ. To start off, look up Colossians 3:1–4.

Being released from the destructive effects of shame is an ongoing battle of faith because we store these feelings in our physical bodies, and Satan will keep using them to try to make us believe his lies of condemnation. He, the accuser of the brethren, is the author of those shaming and condemning messages about our identity. So we need to be prepared to "fight the good fight of faith" (1 Tim. 6:12) and resist the Devil's lies when he uses people and circumstances to push buttons that activate these shame feelings (see James 4:7–8a). We must practice this discipline to retrain our "elephants" and respond to shame feelings differently.

A PRACTICAL EXAMPLE OF A CONVERSATION WITH JESUS ABOUT SHAME

The great challenge we face in being set free from shame is to learn how to make the presence of Jesus real in our experience. Knowing that Jesus is our High Priest with the cognitive part of our brains is one thing; it is something completely different to experience his presence in such a way that we can talk with him as a real person and hear him speak back to us. Many who have practiced experiencing Jesus this way have been able to see him and do things with him. A testimony throughout history is that this spiritual practice can be learned.

So how can we learn this practice? Let me share a modification of a recent technique developed by E. James Wilder and Chris M. Coursey for learning to have a conversation with Jesus.[8]

We will prepare to have this conversation by thinking about a pleasant hill with two comfortable chairs at the top. These two chairs are called the "appreciation memories" and "interactive memories" chairs.[9] We begin by sitting down in the "appreciation memories" chair. When we first sit down, we may experience troubling thoughts and feelings, so our first goal is to calm ourselves. Our goal is to "let the peace of Christ rule in your hearts" (Col. 3:15).

AN EFFECTIVE WAY TO CALM YOURSELF IS AS FOLLOWS:

Take a deep breath from your diaphragm. Then exhale slowly as you say the phrase, "Let the peace of Jesus rule in my heart." Repeat five or six times.

The next step is to remember something you appreciate. It can be a food, an event, or an activity. For example, I appreciate having a dinner date with my wife. I also appreciate Swiss chocolate. Now, focus on the thing you appreciate. Remember the feelings and thoughts that were a part of your appreciation. Finally, let your appreciation experience lead you to express gratitude to Jesus for giving you this experience. Often as we give thanks to Jesus for this gift we appreciate, we become aware of his love for us and his desire to care for us. When this occurs, we have changed seats. We are now sitting in the "interactive memories" chair. We are practicing the presence of Jesus.

When you sense the presence of Jesus, you can begin conversing with him. It is good to begin by talking about pleasant things—ways in which your life has been blessed by Jesus, by friends he has given you, or by pleasant experiences he has provided. Pause in your conversations and let Jesus respond to you.

At this point, how do we know we are hearing a response from Jesus? Very few people actually hear an audible voice booming out, "This is the Lord speaking." To recognize Jesus speaking to us, we need to remind ourselves of the nature of Hebrew poetry. Hebrew poetry does not rhyme words; it rhymes thoughts. Consider Psalm 103:1. "Bless the Lord, O my soul, and all that is within me, bless His holy name." Notice the repeated thoughts. For the psalmist, "O my soul" and "all that is within me" are rhymed thoughts.

In our conversation with Jesus, we may have a thought suddenly come to us. This may be the Lord speaking back to us. Is there a way to test this? Yes, we apply the peace test of Colossians 3:15. "Let the peace of Christ rule in your hearts." The word *rule* can be translated "referee." In our conversation with Jesus, when we receive a thought, we meditate on it. As we meditate, do we experience more peace or less? If we experience more peace, the thought most probably came from Jesus.

After we have learned to experience the presence of Jesus as our High Priest and to converse with him, we can take the next step and talk to him about a painful shame experience.[9] To take this next step, we need to hold on to the presence of Jesus and invite him to go with us into our shame experience. The psalmist did something like this in Psalm 31:1–2. "In you, O Lord, I have taken refuge; let me never be ashamed; in Your righteousness deliver me. Incline Your ear to me, rescue me quickly; be to me a rock of strength, a stronghold to save me."

As you hold onto Jesus, share the event that caused your shame. Invite Jesus into it and talk about all your feelings and thoughts that accompany these feelings of shame. Then wait and let Jesus respond to you. Let yourself see what he does. Apply the peace test to any thoughts that come to you. If you can see his face, what expression do you see? Let him guide your experience from that point on.

Learning to have this conversation with Jesus takes time and practice. Don't get discouraged if this connection doesn't work out as you would like the first time. If you have a friend with whom you can talk about these things, find a time to practice talking to Jesus together. Then you can help each other when difficulties arise.

A SUMMARY OF TOPICS IN CONVERSATIONS WITH JESUS ABOUT SHAME

Some of you may find that having some structure for your conversation with Jesus is helpful. Below is a list of the topics we have discussed about shame in this chapter. In your interactions with Jesus as your High Priest, you may want to select one or more of these topics to share. Figure 3-2 can help you remember some of these things.

1. Jesus, help me to understand how you took my shame on the cross.
2. Does my shame come about because of my sinful acts? Help me to confess them and receive your cleansing.
3. Jesus, have I developed some "broken cisterns" to establish my own identity? Help me to repent from this behavior and renounce them.
4. What part of my shame comes because of the sins of others against me? Show me how to process that kind of shame.
5. Help me to receive by faith my new identity as your child. Remind me of all the good things you say about me. Help me to rejoice and celebrate my new identity.
6. Give me strength and courage to fight the ongoing battle of faith and stand against the lies attached to my shame feelings.

DEPOSITING INTERACTIVE MEMORIES IN THE MEMORY BANKS OF OUR BRAINS

We have spent a lot of time describing the details of having a conversation with Jesus. Each time we have one of these conversations, we create a new interactive memory. It is important that we deposit these interactive memories in the memory banks of our brains. The more of them we have, the more intimate our relationship with Jesus becomes. We can store these interactive memories in our brains by speaking about them to someone else.[10]

TRAINING OUR ELEPHANTS TO SERVE GOD'S PURPOSES

By learning the discipline of practicing the presence of Jesus and conversing with him about our emotions, we begin the process of retraining our elephants. By conversing with Jesus about our shame feelings, these feelings are now moving us toward God instead of moving us to hide from him. Our conversations then give us strength no longer to live according to the lies our shame feelings bring about our identity. Instead we are freed to move in our new identity to serve God and accomplish his purposes in the world.

In the next chapter, we will apply the skills we have learned to fear, then move to anger in Chapter 5.

FOUR

FROM FEAR TO FAITH

When I am afraid, I will put my trust in You.

PSALM 56:3

I sought the Lord, and He answered me, and delivered me from all my fears.

PSALM 34:4

The Lord is my light and my salvation; whom shall I fear? The Lord is the defense of my life; whom shall I dread?

PSALM 27:1

In 1961, I was a postdoctoral research fellow at the California Institute of Technology. I believed God had called me to be an "informal missionary" on a university campus, and it was time for me to take my first interview trip. I had scheduled two interviews on the East Coast, one at Harvard University and another at the University of Massachusetts.

On these trips, one spends most of the day in interviews with professors, and then in the afternoon one gives a seminar on his or her research. At that time, the Chemistry Department at Harvard University was one of the most prestigious in the country, and I knew when I gave my seminar that at least three Nobel Prize winners would be in the audience.

When the time came, I was petrified with fear. Troubling thoughts raced through my mind. *How could someone who stutters ever think he could be a university professor? Why did I agree to interview at Harvard? When I start to speak, am I going to be able to say anything?*

I managed to finish my seminar but experienced lots of blocks in my speech. I was very discouraged and felt much shame because I couldn't communicate like I wanted to. If you have seen the movie *The King's Speech* and identified with the king during his first attempt at a public speech, you will have some idea of how I felt. This story illustrates how fear tempted me to give up doing something I believed God had called me to do.

In this chapter, I want to explore ways fear impacts our lives and give practical ways Jesus, functioning as our High Priest, can help us live so fear doesn't dominate us. Fear is one of the major movers of our old-man elephants. Retraining our elephants to serve Jesus means we must learn how to work with our fears.

Brain scientists tell us the fight-or-flight response is one of the responses hardwired into our brains. Depending on the nature of the stimulus and our genetic disposition, dangerous situations activate parts of our brains that stimulate either fear or anger. When fleeing or withdrawing is appropriate, we identify this emotion as fear (the flight response). When fighting is appropriate, we experience this feeling as anger (the fight response).

This fight-or-flight response is one God has built into our brains to protect us from the dangers we are exposed to in the process of living. Because of the fall, fear or anger stimulated by this response often hinders us from a full life or moves us to destructive actions or attitudes.

To review all that has been written about fear and the ways we might respond to it is beyond the scope of this book. Instead, I want to focus on four categories of fear and provide a biblical foundation for understanding and working with each. The four categories are the following:

1. Appropriate human fear that warns us of danger.
2. Fear that keeps us from entering into the fullness of life. In a Christian context, this could be fear that keeps us from obeying God.
3. Anxiety, a category of fear that has become epidemic in our modern age.
4. The fear of the Lord, a special category of fear the Bible encourages.

APPROPRIATE HUMAN FEAR THAT WARNS US OF DANGER

Fear is a valuable emotion and a gift of God when it warns us of danger we need to avoid. When we think about walking alone at night in a strange city, hopefully we will experience fear. This fear is appropriate and helpful because walking alone at night in a strange city is dangerous. Our bodies send a warning signal to us. This signal moves us to avoid acting on our impulses or to take necessary precautions, such as asking some friends to go with us. Similarly, if we are surfing or skiing and see that the waves are too high or the slopes too steep, we feel fear. This feeling warns us that these situations may lead to harm. Fear is a message encouraging us to think carefully before we participate.

Fear That Keeps Us from Entering the Fullness of Life

This category of fear is the one that gives us the most trouble. We have fears that keep us from doing things we desire or experiencing life in its fullness. For Christians, this category of fear can keep us from doing what God has called us to do. The story of my interview at Harvard is an example of how my fear tempted me to doubt God's calling on my life.

One function all emotions play in our lives is that they are messengers. Learning to read the messages our emotions bring is an important skill we must learn that helps us understand and manage our emotions. When we experience fear, we must ask ourselves, "What is the danger stimulating my fear?" For example, I have to ask myself this question whenever I receive an invitation to speak in a new situation.

Let me describe the sequence of thoughts that helps me answer this question. This sequence didn't come to me all at once; assembling it took several years. But here's the breakdown.

1. The danger is that I will stutter when I speak.
2. If I stutter, my listeners will think I am strange or abnormal.
3. If they think I am strange or abnormal, they won't like me or want to have a relationship with me.
4. My stuttering will distract them, and they won't be able to listen to what I have to say.
5. I will be failing Jesus because I cannot communicate the truth clearly.

When I originally created this list, what became clear to me was that the surface fear of stuttering had deeper fears lying beneath it. Mainly, I feared failure and rejection. A deeper insight came when I realized that the underlying fears I faced were all related to shame. They all had to do with falling short of the expectations of my "ideal self."

In the last chapter we pointed out that these shame feelings can be very painful. A way to summarize all of these fears is to say, "If I stutter, I will experience painful shame feelings, and these feelings will bring along with them all the thoughts of failure that are tied to them." This is the real danger associated with my fear of stuttering. This is what makes me want to run away from experiences that provoke this danger.

People who stutter aren't the only ones who fear public speaking. A number of surveys have found that public speaking is one of the greatest fears for many. Jerry Seinfeld, an American comedian, got a big laugh when he joked about a survey that ranked fear of public speaking as being greater than fear of death. "In other words," he deadpanned, "at a funeral, the average person would rather be in the casket than giving the eulogy."[1] Seinfeld's joke pretty well describes my feelings when I gave my interview speech at Harvard.

Reflection Exercise

Make a list of some of your greatest fears. Rank them in order of strength. Read through this list and ask yourself some questions (if you wish, you can make this another example of a conversation with Jesus). "How has this fear kept me from experiencing the fullness of life?" "How has this fear prevented me from considering or entering into activities God might be calling me into?"

FEAR AND EXCITEMENT

In Chapter 2, one of the worldview questions we asked was, "What was God's purpose in creation?" I would like us to do some creative speculation by asking, "In creation, what was God's purpose for the emotion we now experience as fear?" I believe we can find part of the answer to this question when we consider the relationship between fear and excitement.

Physiological studies have shown that the hormonal response leading to these two emotions is almost identical. In both cases our adrenal glands give us a dose of adrenaline. Add to this idea the activities people do for excitement. Most involve doing something that may inspire fear. Skiing, surfing, bungee jumping, parasailing, rock climbing—all these activities are exciting because each requires an element of overcoming fear.

Excitement moves people to test themselves against nature and extend the limits of their experience. When we think about going on an adventure, we get excited, and the feeling of excitement motivates us to enter into the adventure. This connection between fear and excitement will be important when we talk about responding to our fears.

God created us with the capacity for excitement. He is a God of adventure. Think about the world he created with all its opportunities to do exciting things. Of course, when we ask how our fallenness has affected this purpose, we see that excitement isn't always good. It can, in fact, become an addiction. Our modern age is discovering the destructive effects of too much adrenaline stimulation due to the drive of many to constantly seek excitement.[2]

ANXIETY

We need to consider this third category of fear separately because in our modern Western society, anxiety has become a major problem. The problem is complex because developments in modern culture have led to a whole spectrum of anxiety disorders. The spectrum extends from simple worry to panic-anxiety disorder, characterized by panic attacks that seem to come from nowhere. The many different ways people experience anxiety in modern life has led Dr. Archibald Hart to distinguish two different types of anxiety. He calls them "worry anxiety" and "endogenous anxiety."[3] They are different in that "worry anxiety" comes mainly from thoughts in our minds, while malfunctions in our brain chemistry and/or genetic factors drive "endogenous anxiety."

In the remainder of this book, I will talk more about "worry anxiety." As Dr. Hart points out, the stimulus for this type of anxiety comes from *within our minds* rather than from an external stimulus or out-of-balance brain chemistry. The dangers, therefore, arise in our imaginations. We can discover anxiety producers by listening to thoughts in our minds that begin with the phrase "what if."

My wife and I travel a lot, and I frequently find myself thinking, *What if the airport bus gets stuck in traffic and we don't get to the airport on time?*

What if the plane is late and I miss my connection? In this age of economic uncertainties, many are wondering, *What if I lose my job? What if I can't make my mortgage payment?* These thoughts are all tightly bound to feelings of anxiety.

The strength of this feeling may vary depending on the person and circumstances. When these feelings come to you, examine the thoughts going through your mind. See if "what ifs" are attacking your thinking.

Understanding a little more about the physiology of fear and anxiety is important. The adrenal glands produce two major hormones: adrenaline and cortisol. Adrenaline is quick acting and gives us the sudden surge of physiological effects associated with the fight-or-flight response. For example, Sarah and I were walking along a highway in Kona, Hawaii, when suddenly a car swerved up behind us and the driver gave a loud blast of his horn. In an instant, both Sarah and I experienced an internal panic response and leaped closer to the side of the road. The car, filled with laughing kids, passed us; they were obviously having fun at our expense. We had experienced the effects of a quick shot of adrenaline, which had activated our flight-or-fight response. The effects of adrenaline act and wear off quickly. A couple of minutes later, after our pulse rate and breathing returned to normal, we continued our walk.

Cortisol, a slower-acting hormone, increases our vigilance and prepares our body to respond to a danger that might occur. It is one of the major hormones stimulated by stress, which almost always brings anxiety along for the ride. Stress often has to do with longer-term dangers we don't know how to respond to.

Our bodies need cortisol to increase our ability to respond to situations that haven't happened yet. If a resting or calming period follows the stress, the body properly adjusts to the cortisol. Chronic anxiety or stress, however, keeps the blood levels of cortisol high for long periods of time, a condition numerous studies have shown to bring serious health consequences. So learning how to cope with our anxiety and stress is important.[4]

THE FEAR OF THE LORD

One of the important contributions YWAM has made to our understanding of living as Christians concerns the fear of the Lord. Discipleship-training courses taught around the world encourage students to study and meditate on Scripture passages about this fear. This is a good kind of fear the Scriptures actually encourage us to have. The Hebrew word all Old Testament passages use for the fear of the Lord can also be translated "reverence."

My wife and I were fascinated with this teaching when we attended YWAM's discipleship training course in 1983. I have continued to reflect on how the fear of the Lord fits into other truths I have been learning about fear. Specifically, how is the fear of the Lord similar to, or different from, other fears I experience? I began to find an answer to this question when in our course we heard Joy Dawson teach about the verse "The fear of the Lord is to hate evil" (Prov. 8:13). In this lecture, she linked hating evil with feeling disgust when we encounter evil. One dimension of the fear of the Lord is to seek revelation from God about how to train our elephants to feel disgust when we come into contact with evil.

Brain research has shown that disgust is one of the core feelings God has designed our brains to experience.[5] In light of our worldview considerations, God's original purpose for disgust was that it would provide an emotion that would move us *away* from evil. The effect of the fall was that our emotions were perverted so that instead of experiencing disgust in the presence of evil, we experience attraction. God's purpose in redemption is to restore our capacity to experience disgust when we come into contact with evil.

In the New Testament, we find a number of situations God commands us to flee from—for example, immorality (1 Cor. 6:18), idolatry (10:14), and youthful lusts (2 Tim. 2:22). These are examples of evil for which disgust is the appropriate emotion. In these situations, the fear of the Lord, which includes disgust with evil, recognizes the danger spoken of in these examples. We need it to motivate the flight response. We need the fear of the Lord in our life journeys as well. It helps us learn how to resist our fallen emotions that *attract* us to evil. In our conversations with Jesus we need to ask him to increase the fear of the Lord that moves us to feel disgust for, or to hate, evil. This is the key to empowering us to avoid the Internet porn site or to switch the channel—to flee things that stimulate lust. To find this strength we need more reverence and awe of the holiness and power of God. More fear of the Lord will make us disgusted with evil and warn us of the dangers of flirting with it.

As I continued to ponder the fear of the Lord in my own experience, I became convinced that this fear must contain a positive element. Proverbs 14:27 says, "The fear of the Lord is a fountain of life, that one may avoid the snares of death." The positive and negative elements of the fear of the Lord came together for me when I read a story by John Piper, a Baptist pastor in Minnesota.[6] He told the story in conjunction with his meditation on Psalm 147:11. "But the Lord takes pleasure in those who fear him, in those who hope in his steadfast love" (RSV).

We learned earlier that Hebrew poetry rhymes thoughts rather than words. Using this idea, we must conclude that this verse means that fearing the Lord and hoping in his steadfast love are two different pictures of the same reality. To illustrate this truth, John Piper used a story to show how the two parts of this verse fit together. The following story is my elaboration of his idea.

A Story Illustrating the Fear of the Lord

Greenland is a land of icy mountains, where many people go for adventure. It is also a land of fierce storms with ice, wind, and snow. To be caught on the side of a glacier during one of those storms would mean certain death.

In your imagination visualize climbing a steep glacier in Greenland. The day begins sunny, and you enjoy the exhilaration of the climb along with the beauty of the environment. Suddenly, as you gaze at an ice formation in the distance, you become aware of a huge storm with lightning, wind, and ice approaching rapidly from behind you. You feel panic because you know that if you don't find shelter, you are finished. Your only hope is to keep climbing and hope you will find a place of safety.

Just as the storm is about to hit, you see a crevice in the ice that looks big enough for you to get into. After you squeeze into the crevice, you discover a lovely ice cave. You enter the ice cave just as the storm hits. As you realize you're safe, your adrenaline reaction calms down. You look at the lightning flashes and listen to the wind howling outside, but you feel secure. In fact, while in the safety of the ice cave, you can enjoy the storm in all its awesome power. (Have you ever been inside a cozy house by a warm fire when a fierce storm raged outside? What feelings did you have?)

John Piper points out that this experiential picture describes what God is saying in this verse. The fear of the Lord is the awareness of his awesome power, holiness, and majesty. That is what the storm represents. Hoping in his steadfast love is the knowledge that he alone can provide the place of safety and security for us. The ice cave or cozy fire represents this truth. God is delighted and takes pleasure when we experience him in this twofold way. Having the emotions of fear and hope in our hearts simultaneously makes up the fear of the Lord. I'm trying to discover how to grow in experiencing this kind of "stereo emotion" in my own personal life.

The important message is that we need to ask Jesus to increase the strength of our fear of him. We desperately need more of this kind of fear.

Responding to Our Fears

How does Scripture teach us to respond to our fears? Let's apply the things we learned about emotions in Chapter 2. Postulate two proposed that primary emotions are not sinful. This means we must not regard the feeling of fear as evil or sinful. We must accept or embrace the fact that we are afraid. This may be difficult for two reasons. First, there is a teaching in some Christian circles that implies if we're really spiritual, we're not supposed to experience fear or anxiety. This teaching encourages us to *deny* our fears, not acknowledge them.

Second, as we have seen, fear brings with it a temptation to withdraw from various life experiences. But when we withdraw, we feel weak. I always felt like a weakling when my fear of stuttering kept me from doing something I really wanted to do. We don't like the idea of being weak, and this thinking encourages us to deny our fears. These two reasons conspire to keep us from acknowledging our fears.

Postulate four in Chapter 2 reminds us that Jesus, as our Great High Priest, wants to be with us when we're afraid; therefore, we can use our fears to move us to have a conversation with Jesus. This is a concrete personal application of the passage we read at the beginning of this chapter. "When I am afraid, I will put my trust in You" (Ps. 56:3).

When we look at Scripture, we find that the antidote for the destructive effects of fear is God's presence. The Psalms, a great resource for those who are afraid, speak of God countless times as our refuge, fortress, and stronghold. I believe the reason there are so many of these passages is because God knows we will face many dangers in life—some real and some imagined. Dangers bring fear, so we need a place of safety to flee to when we face such dangers. The next Reflection Exercise can help us meditate on how coming to God as our refuge and fortress is the antidote for facing danger. All the images used in these passages from Psalms picture God as a place of safety.

Reflection Exercise

Look up each of the following verses and write them down in a single paragraph: Psalms 9:9; 31:2–3; 56:3–4; 59:16; 62:6. Read through the paragraph you wrote and list circumstances in which the Psalms encourage us to experience God as our refuge.

Conversing with Jesus about our fears is the key to keep fear from moving us to withdraw from the fullness of life or to disobey God. Fear-motivated withdrawal can lead to a sense of helplessness and perhaps eventually hopelessness and depression. By developing a habit of conversing with Jesus when we are afraid, we actually begin to experience the redemption of our fears. Our fears now move us to God rather than move us to hide from him and withdraw from life.

Let's recall our discussion about the relationship between fear and excitement. The message we receive in the Psalms is that the presence of God is the antidote for our fears. Applying this truth to our personal experience means bringing the presence of Jesus with us into an event we fear. The story of Moses sending the spies into the Promised Land gives us an example of this. When the ten spies reported after coming back from their mission, they looked at the giants in the land and the walled cities and said, "There is no way we can conquer the land" (Num. 13:31–33, my paraphrase). But Joshua and Caleb said, "The land is rich beyond belief. Don't be afraid. *The Lord is with us* and has taken their protection away" (Num. 14:6–9, my paraphrase and emphasis). The knowledge that the presence of the Lord would go with them led Joshua and Caleb to see entering the land as an adventure. Their fear turned to excitement.

What about the strongest fear on your list? If you were convinced that Jesus was going with you into that situation, what changes would take place in your emotions?

Conversing with Jesus about Our Fears

To have a conversation with Jesus about our fears, we want to follow the same procedure as when we talked with him about our shame—except now the subject is fear. I encourage you to review that section in the last chapter about establishing a relational connection with Jesus.

The first step is to find a quiet place and sit in the appreciation memories chair. Contemplate the thing you appreciate until your appreciation becomes gratitude and you sense Jesus is with you. Then speak to him and tell him you want to talk with him about your fears. You may pick one of the fears from your list or ask Jesus to show you a fear he wants you to work on.

The best way to proceed is to let Jesus lead the conversation from that point on, but doing so might be difficult if you're learning how to have these conversations for the first time. For that reason, I have provided a sample conversation you may wish to follow to help you get started. Feel free to change directions as Jesus leads you. Remember to let the peace of Jesus be your referee throughout the process. It you come to a place where you have lost this peace, return to the appreciation memories chair and reestablish the connection with Jesus.

A Sample Conversation with Jesus about Fear

Thank you, Lord, that you are my Great High Priest and that you want to be with me when I am afraid. (This is an "appreciation statement." You may want to add other things about Jesus you appreciate. Continue to sit in the "appreciation memories" chair when you do this.)

Lord, right now I'm afraid to _____ or of _____ (name what you are afraid of and share how strong the fear is), and this fear is keeping me from _____ (name the goal the fear is preventing you from achieving.).

Help me, Lord, to see and name the danger that is stimulating my fear. (Pause to let Jesus bring insights into your heart and mind.)

Lord, I want to come to you as my refuge, my fortress, and my stronghold, and I ask you to help me keep a sense of your presence so I can know I'm safe. (Apply the peace test we discussed earlier.) Then, Lord, I ask you to help me look at the danger I face with your eyes. (Pause again to let Jesus speak to your heart about how his presence might change how you see the danger.)

Lord, how do you want me to respond to this danger? Is this something I need to flee? Or is my fear keeping me from experiencing the fullness of life you intend me to have? Is my fear keeping me from obeying you? Is my fear keeping me in a state of ongoing anxiety? (Wait in the presence of the Lord until you believe you have some answers.)

Lord, if I'm missing the fullness of life because of my fears, then I ask that you would help me know how to invite you to be present with me as I face doing the thing I fear.

Lord, I want to learn to experience your presence as the answer for my fears! Help me to see that when you are with me, facing the danger can become an adventure, and you can change my experience into one of excitement. (Try to form a mental picture of the Lord with you as you do the thing you fear. See what happens to your feelings as you focus on that mental picture.)

Lord, I thank you that I am learning a new way to respond when I feel fear. I ask you specifically to let my feelings of fear be a strong reminder to come to you and talk with you about my fears. In this way, help me to stop avoiding my fears but to explore them and discover a deeper relationship with you in the process. I thank you for Psalm 34:4. "I sought the Lord, and He answered me, and delivered me from all my fears."

Anxiety Revisited

The sample conversation above focuses on talking with Jesus about a fear that keeps us from entering the fullness of life or obeying God. Let's now look at how the situation is different when we deal with anxiety.

Often when I talk about anxiety, someone asks, "Doesn't the Bible say we're not supposed to be anxious? Isn't it sinful to be anxious?" Let's examine the Scriptures to see if we can answer this question. In Matthew 6:25–34, Jesus told us specifically that we shouldn't worry or be anxious. Jesus was clearly talking about "worry anxiety" here. We hear the same message from Paul in Philippians 4:6–7. "Be anxious for nothing, but in everything by prayer and supplication with thanksgiving let your requests be made known to God. And the peace of God, which surpasses all comprehension, will guard your hearts and your minds in Christ Jesus."

These two passages make it clear that ongoing anxiety is not pleasing to God because it moves us away from trusting him to provide the things we need. But these two passages are in the Bible because both Jesus and Paul knew all of us would experience anxious thoughts.

Having an anxious thought come into our minds, however, is not sinful. It's when we dwell on these anxious thoughts that we fall into sin because our anxious thoughts take us further and further away from trusting God. I prefer to believe Jesus and Paul gave these instructions because they knew all of us would struggle with anxiety. They taught us what to do when we experienced it. Jesus told us to "put away anxious thoughts" (Matt. 6:25 NEB) and to focus on "set[ting] [our] mind[s] on God's kingdom and his justice" (Matt. 6:33 NEB).

We need to learn how to train our anxious thoughts so they will move us to a deeper trust in God. Paul tells us to respond to anxious thoughts by prayer and supplication (Phil. 4:6). (Does that sound like a conversation with Jesus?) As we respond this way, we receive "the peace of God…that will 'guard your hearts and your minds'" (Phil. 4:7). This is another example of how we should train our elephants.

Do you remember the story about our lost tote bag at the beginning of this book? My anxiety level was super high because of the "what if" thoughts racing through my mind, especially the thought, *What if the conductor comes and finds out we don't have tickets?* I mentioned that Sarah and I found a seat, talked, and had a conversation with Jesus. My panic began to subside, and we experienced the peace promised in the passage above.

During my conversation with Jesus, he brought back to my mind a part of my teaching—that to deal with "what if" statements, we need to remove the "what" and focus on a specific action we will take "if" the thing we fear happens. I decided that if the conductor asked for my ticket, I would tell him that my tickets were in a tote bag that was missing when we boarded the train. (We presumed that someone had stolen it.) I would offer to pay for new tickets. Making this plan of action further reduced my anxiety level. In addition it gave me an argument to use against my thoughts when I was tempted to bring the "what if" back. Sarah and I committed ourselves to God.

A miraculous thing happened on that trip. We rode three different Swiss trains that day. In each one the conductor came, passed us by, and never asked for our tickets. We have ridden trains in Switzerland many times, and the conductors have always asked to see our tickets.

Another reason why initial feelings of anxiety are not sinful is that some anxiety arises because of basic tendencies God has built into our brains; these are a normal part of living. Children have two basic tendencies that guide their development. One is the need to explore (curiosity is an expression of this tendency), and the other is the need to find safety. We can see these two needs interacting by thinking of a child just learning to walk. Imagine a father kneeling a few feet away from a toddler who is just learning to walk. He holds out his arms and says, "Come to Daddy." The mother helps the child to stand up and says, "Walk to Daddy."

We can see the tension between these two needs by looking at the child's body language. He wants to launch out on this new adventure, but he also wants to stay safe with his mother. Because of this dilemma, the child experiences anxiety. The first time he tries to walk, he may feel insecure and run back to his mother. The need for safety wins. The child feels peace and security there. Eventually, however, the need to explore triumphs, and the child walks to his father. When that happens, the child and his parents experience joy.

The tension the child feels in the above situation is an example of "normal anxiety." The anxiety is resolved when the child makes a "specific choice." He can choose either safety or adventure. In the one case the child experiences peace in the safety of his mother's arms. In the other case the child experiences adventure by accomplishing the new task.

We will continue to experience the tension between these two "needs" as we age. We experience this tension as normal anxiety. However, we live in a world that is fallen, one that has become so driven that no opportunity for rest and recovery after an exhilarating experience exists. In this world the stresses of life can transform normal anxiety into "toxic anxiety."

In normal anxiety we commit ourselves to a course of action. We choose either exploration or safety. Then, after the choice, we experience a rest and recovery period. In toxic anxiety we are unable to choose an action, so we ruminate (go over something in our minds again and again), imagining possible outcomes to our situation. There is no rest and recovery period when we experience peace. This rumination becomes sinful anxiety. It may eventually develop into "endogenous anxiety."

So let's return to applying Philippians 4:6–7. I believe prayer and supplication mentioned in these verses are identical to having a conversation with God about our anxieties. We need revelation to be able to name and assess the danger lying behind our anxiety. We need to see if there is any action we can take. The result of conversing with Jesus about our anxious thoughts is that he helps us formulate an action appropriate to the situation. If there is no possible action we can take, he then encourages us to trust him as our fortress and place of safety.

Writing about the process make it sound easy, but it isn't. Worry anxiety can become a thought habit we must overcome by discipline and practice.[7]

The important message is that, while learning how to experience Jesus as our Great High Priest and have conversations with him about our fears, we experience the truth of the Psalms passages listed at the beginning of this chapter.

When I am afraid, I will put my trust in You. (Ps. 56:3)

I sought the Lord, and He answered me, and delivered me from all my fears. (Ps. 34:4)

The Lord is my light and my salvation; whom shall I fear? The Lord is the defense of my life; whom shall I dread? (Ps. 27:1)

Many people who have been in the classes I taught about emotions have commented that they desire to have a more intimate relationship with God. Intimacy with another person grows when we share things from our hearts with him or her. By learning how to share about our fears with Jesus, we discover that we move into a more intimate relationship with him.

In the next chapter, we will tackle the question of how to keep anger from becoming destructive and instead use it to move us into a deeper relationship with God.

FIVE

ANGER: DEADLY SIN OR GIFT FROM GOD?

He who is slow to anger is better than the mighty, and he who rules his spirit than he who captures a city.

PROVERBS 16:32

Of all the core emotions, anger is both the most controversial and most difficult to deal with. Libraries offer loads of books about anger, and the Bible is full of references to it. Theologians living in monasteries in the fourth through seventh centuries considered anger one of the "seven deadly sins."[1] A modern Jewish psychotherapist writes that helping his clients overcome the destructive effects of anger makes up a large proportion of his practice.[2] We cannot listen to the news without hearing reports of the destructive effects of someone's anger. Road rage, spousal abuse, shootings in schools, and many other acts of violence are modern-day examples of anger fulfilling its role as one of the seven deadly sins.

WORLDVIEW QUESTIONS SPECIFICALLY APPLIED TO ANGER

In Chapter 2 we proposed three biblical worldview questions one might ask of any subject. Then we looked at four postulates about emotions that summarized our answers when we applied these three questions to emotions in general. How do the disturbing facts cited above fit when we apply these postulates to anger?

Anger is one of the core emotions. That means in creation God must have had a good purpose for anger in mind. But we are fallen, and nowhere has the perversion of our emotions become more evident than in the case of anger. In Chapter 2, as an example of the application of our postulates, we told the story of Cain and Abel's sacrifice. Cain was "very angry" (Gen. 4:5), but God was present and invited Cain to talk about his anger. God responded to Cain by pointing out that anger is a very dangerous emotion. He asked Cain to explore why he was angry and told him he must "master it." (You may want to review that section in Chapter 2 or read the whole story in Genesis 4:1–8 again.) God's conversation with Cain indicated that even though Cain felt "very angry," he hadn't yet sinned. We know, however, that Cain was not able to master what his feelings were moving him to do. He ultimately murdered his brother, Abel.

God's Created Purpose for Anger

To understand our experiences of anger, we need to remind ourselves of God's created purpose for emotions. This involves thinking carefully about the second and third postulates described in Chapter 2. God's purpose for all core emotions is that they become the "movers" of our lives. They provide the motivational energy for our actions. To fully understand the operation of emotions in our lives, we must make a distinction between the feeling associated with an emotion and the action or response that emotion moves us to.

In the conversation between God and Cain, God tried to get Cain to see that Cain had the responsibility to choose what kind of action would result from his anger. Paul made this same distinction between emotion and action. In Ephesians 4:26–27, he stated, "If you are angry, do not let anger lead you into sin; do not let sunset find you still nursing it; leave no loophole for the devil" (NEB). Here Paul said we can be angry without sinning; feelings of anger are not in themselves sinful.

Paul also confirmed what God had said to Cain—that anger is a dangerous emotion. Anger has the powerful potential of moving us to a sinful response. Because of this, Paul told us to process our anger as soon as possible. Don't let it hang around and, most important, do not nurse it. To *nurse* means to feed and nurture. Let's keep these facts in mind as we explore another Scripture referring to anger.

A Model for Redeemed Anger

Let's examine a biblical example of feelings of anger that didn't lead to sin. In Mark 3:1–5, we find the story of Jesus healing a man with a withered hand on the Sabbath. If you have a Bible handy, take time to read this whole story. For our purpose, the main point is that in verse 5 we find Jesus "looking around at them with anger." We know from other Scriptures that Jesus didn't sin. Scripture says he did only what he saw the Father do (John 5:19). That means when the Father looked at this situation, he also must have been angry.

Yes, Jesus had the capacity to become angry. As a human being, Jesus used a capacity God had built into humans at creation. In this situation, however, Jesus's anger didn't move him to sin. Instead, what did it move him to do? It moved him to bring healing to a handicapped man. Jesus's anger moved him to perform an action that was an expression of God's love. But Jesus didn't need anger for that purpose.

Compassion would have served just as well. In Mark 1:41, we find compassion moving Jesus to touch and heal a leper. Here Jesus needed anger to accomplish something else. By doing this healing on the Sabbath, he confronted an evil system that had captured the thinking of the Pharisees. This evil system kept people in bondage and treated this man with contempt because he was handicapped. We come to this conclusion by reading the parallel passage, Matthew 12:10–14.

In this passage Jesus added the following question: "What man is there among you who has a sheep, and if it falls into a pit on the Sabbath, will he not take hold of it and lift it out? How much more valuable then is a man than a sheep! So then, it is lawful to do good on the Sabbath." The main point of Jesus's response was that the Pharisees were using their traditions to relegate some people to being less than animals. Their traditions gave them an excuse for contempt. Jesus's anger moved him to confront this unjust system.

Jesus's anger in this situation as well as many references in Scripture to God's anger toward injustice was what led Doctors Allender and Longman to say, "God designed and blessed anger in order to energize our passion to destroy sin."[3] These authors devote two chapters in their book to focusing on the relationship between anger and injustice.[4] The title of the chapter devoted to righteous anger is "Righteous Anger: An Assault against Injustice." Seeing anger as a gift from God to confront injustice helps us understand one of God's present purposes for anger.

Our Experience of Anger: Fallen or Redeemed?

The Scriptures present two basic facts about anger we must keep in mind so we know what to do when we experience it. First, anger is a dangerous emotion. We are exposed to examples of its evil effects every day when we see how fallen anger moves people to destructive actions. Second, the feeling of anger is a God-given capacity that can move people to constructive actions. I have called this "redeemed anger." Allender and Longman refer to this as righteous anger. Our task is to learn how to distinguish these two types of anger.

In the scriptural example from Mark 3, we find that certain conditions must be satisfied before our anger can move us to a "redeemed" action. First, we must be angry at what God is angry about. Second, our feelings of anger must move us to accomplish God's purposes in his way. Anyone who has examined his or her anger experiences has found that these two conditions are rarely satisfied. James described our usual anger situation by saying, "But everyone must be...*slow* to anger; for the anger of man does not achieve the righteousness of God" (James 1:19–20, emphasis mine).

Repression, Denial, and Sublimation: Detouring around Anger

I mentioned in Chapter 1 that I had been out of touch with my emotions for fifty years of my life. In Chapters 2 and 3 you saw that I experienced much shame and fear during those years. My problem was that I had no way of processing those emotions, so I repressed or denied them. My situation with anger was different. If someone had asked me at age fifty what my experience with anger had been, I would have replied that I'd had very few experiences of anger. I remember being angry in only two situations.

As I have studied anger, I have come to the conclusion that anger was the emotion I was most successful in repressing or denying. Angry feelings would come into my awareness only rarely. For example, when I was stuck in traffic and someone passed me illegally on the right and then wanted to cut in later, I felt angry. But these feelings were never strong enough to move me to any kind of reaction to my anger. When I think about my past, I come to the conclusion that I may have had frequent feelings of anger, but

I repressed any impulse to respond to them. This practice, of course, could lead me to deny that I was ever angry.

Another factor at work in my life has influenced my lack of anger; it is another way to respond to emotions. Psychologists call it "sublimation." Sublimation means transforming natural expressions of an impulse into socially acceptable ones. In the social situations in which I grew up, fear and withdrawal were more socially acceptable responses, so I transformed any anger feelings I may have experienced into expressions of fear and withdrawal.

When we dissect an event of anger below, we will discuss sublimation in more detail. As I write this chapter, I'm asking God to help me understand my own anger from the inside out, and he has already begun to do that.

DISSECTING AN EVENT OF ANGER

Here I present some modern treatments of anger to help meet two challenges that are the focus of this chapter. Both challenges come out of our study of God's conversation with Cain in Genesis 4. The first challenge is to answer the question, "Why are you angry?" The second challenge is to respond to God's injunction to Cain that he must master his impulses driven by his feeling of anger. We will discover that a key to both challenges is to learn to have a conversation with Jesus about our anger.

To help us meet these challenges, let's explore what happens to us when we get angry. Consider Figure 5-1.[5] The experience of anger is initiated by an event that happens and presents data to our brains. This is represented by circle number one, the Incident circle. This event can be outside us in our environment or inside us—a memory or thought that comes to mind or a feeling in some part of our bodies.

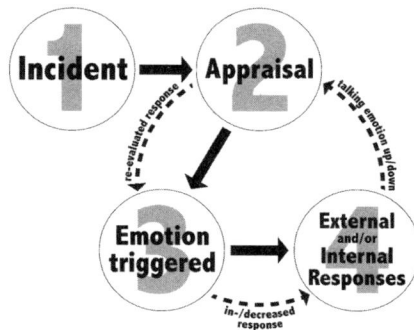

Figure 5-1

We probably have no difficulty thinking of events that happen outside of us. For example, suppose you have been waiting for some time in the checkout line at the grocery store. Suddenly another checkout clerk arrives to work at the next cash register, but she grabs the cart of the person *behind* you to start her line. You instantly feel angry. What responses might you have?

Here's an example of an internal stimulus. Suppose you are peacefully going about your day when you remember someone saying something hurtful to you. Suddenly you feel anger toward that person.

As the data from circle number one enters our brains, it goes immediately to circle number two and undergoes an evaluation process. This evaluation process may be a cognitive event in which you are aware that the process is going on, or it might be automatic, stimulated by the limbic system of your brain. In this latter case your brain makes a decision that danger exists without your conscious involvement. When this evaluation process determines that the input data warrants an emotional response, the mind sends a signal to parts of the brain that control hormonal release, and you experience emotions. Our emotions always include a physiological response mediated by a hormonal release from the adrenal glands (corresponding to circle number three in Figure 5-1).

At this point we can better understand sublimation. The brain response activated when the valuing system detects danger is called the fight-or-flight response. Our life experiences have conditioned our emotional responses to this danger. If the appropriate response is to fight, our "needed" emotion is anger. If the appropriate response is to flee, our "needed" emotion is fear. The social situations present in each person's developmental history will determine his or her "needed" emotion. My learned reaction to dangerous situations was fear. That is why it is difficult for me to experience anger.

We know emotions move us to some kind of response. Circle number four in Figure 5-1 represents this. Again, this response may be external or internal. In the case of anger, an external response might be to shout, stamp our feet, or slam a door. An internal response might be to seethe, become resentful, or plot revenge.

One of the advantages of this analysis of an experience of anger is that we can begin to see where introducing change is possible. First, we must recognize that we have very little to no power to change circle number one.

Most of the initiating events that stimulate anger are outside our control. People will continue to crowd into line, and anger-producing thoughts will continue to come unbidden into our minds. An exception to this lack of power to change circle number one may be when the environmental stimulus comes from a *repeated* pattern of abuse or disrespect. Then we may find some power to stop the repetitive pattern, but that gets ahead of our story because it involves a planned constructive response (circle number four) on our part.

Once we get to circle number three, we have little power to change the emotional response directly. The only way to bring change here is through drugs or medication. Drugs, alcohol, or medication affects the whole emotional response system. For some anger situations, where anger is too frequent or too intense, using medications to dampen the anger response and enable other interventions to succeed may be necessary. What's important to see is that dampening the emotional response does nothing to help us understand how the valuing process links the stimulus to the need for an emotional response. Drugs or medications do not help us answer the question, "Why are you angry?"

That leaves circles number two and number four as possible change points. To change our external response to the feelings, we need to use our ability to choose—our wills. Most of our responses to anger are learned habits, which we can change by practicing different responses.

One piece of advice for dealing with anger has been around for a long time and is actually a good one. Count to ten before you respond. This is an action you can choose to do. Counting to ten gives you time to think about the consequences of your actions. It also gives a little time for the initial emotional surge, due to hormonal release, to subside. Choosing to have a conversation with Jesus about your anger before acting on it is also an example of how to use your will.

The Scriptures affirm these two responses. "He who is slow to anger is better than the mighty, and he who rules his spirit, than he who captures a city" (Prov. 16:32). Pondering this passage makes it clear that the writer is talking about being slow to express or respond to feelings of anger. If the verse were talking about being slow to *feel* anger, there wouldn't be any need to be "mighty" or to rule our spirits. Counting to ten and conversing with

Jesus are disciplines that make us slow to respond to our anger.

Choosing to dialogue with Jesus or to look at our internal responses to feelings takes us to circle number two. I believe this is the most important circle for affecting change in our experiences of anger. When we explore the sources of our anger, we are working in circle number two. That was what God wanted Cain to do when he asked him why he was angry. The process of conversing with Jesus is working in circle number two. We will explore this process in a later section.

In Figure 5-1, you will notice dashed lines connecting circles two, three, and four. These dashed lines indicate feedback loops. Let's talk about the feedback between our external/internal responses, circle number four, and circle number two. When we look at the Scriptures about anger, we learn that it is dangerous to "nurse" our anger (see Eph. 4:26 NEB). If we choose to hold onto our anger and tell ourselves all the reasons we are right to be angry, then we have an experience of "talking up" our anger. This feedback to circle number two then activates the feedback loop between circles number two and three, and feelings of anger get stronger. Or we can choose to "talk down" our anger. In this case we explore other explanations of the situation we do not perceive as attacking us. In this case feedback between circles number two and number three decreases the intensity of our angry feelings.

An American group, Alternatives to Violence, works with perpetrators of domestic violence. One skill this group teaches is recognizing when we talk up our anger and learning how to talk it down. One myth about anger is that strong, overt expressions of anger help to get rid of it. The truth is that these overt expressions only make expressing anger easier the next time.

Our responses to anger can become habits. The more we practice a habit, the more ingrained it becomes. Recent brain research has shown that the prefrontal cortex plays an important role in managing our emotions. Counting to ten or conversing with Jesus strengthens the ability of the prefrontal cortex to manage our impulses. Practicing overt expressions of anger weakens this ability.

Anger as a Response to Primary Pain

Dr. Neil Clark Warren has proposed another treatment of anger that will help us meet our two challenges. He stated, "Anger is a God-given gift that allows your body to take action to get rid of the pain in your life."[6] He sees anger as a "messenger" that tells us our bodies are responding to a danger; we need to look at that danger. Dr. Warren tries to help us answer the question, "Why are you angry?" The answer he gives is that in the course of living, we have had experiences our brains have labeled as painful. He wants to answer the question, "Why are you angry?" by encouraging us to explore the nature of this pain. In Dr. Warren's model, this pain precipitates the anger, and the anger then moves us to various responses.

I have constructed a diagram based on Dr. Warren's recorded lecture

Figure 5-2

(Figure 5-2) that summarizes his ideas. I have added to this diagram the theme of this book—that feelings of anger can move us to have a conversation with Jesus. See if you can associate the parts of Figure 5-2 with the various circles in Figure 5-1. Figure 5-2 illustrates the possible responses we can have to feelings of anger. Dr. Warren talks about seven negative responses. I have added "Conversation with Jesus" as a positive response. Let's briefly look at each of these responses. We will begin with the negative ones.

AGGRESSION

Aggression is a way of acting that brings harm to someone or something. Slamming the door of your car when it won't start, calling someone names when he or she attacks you, throwing a chair at a referee at a sporting event when you don't like his or her call—these are all examples of aggression. Of course, abuse in all its forms is aggression. Aggression is an outward response to anger.

HOSTILITY, HATRED

Hostility is negative thinking about people or situations; it's an example of an inward response to anger. Blaming is often a symptom of hostility. When hostility increases, it can become hatred, which is a wish or desire for someone or something not to exist. Hatred also involves an extreme dislike or revulsion for something or someone. It can lead to murder, which is an action that destroys the hated person or thing. In this case, an inner response—hostility—has led to an outward response: aggression.

MALICE, CONTEMPT

Contempt is an attitude of disrespect accompanied by a feeling of intense dislike. Contempt can lead to regarding someone as vile or worthless. We mentioned that the Pharisees were contemptuous of the man with the withered hand, whom Jesus healed in the synagogue.

Malice is enmity of heart or ill will toward another. It is a deep-seated dislike that takes delight when bad things happen to someone. Notice that malice is an attitude that is the opposite of love; love is an attitude of heart that wishes good for another. Malice is one of the attitudes Christians should "put away" (Eph. 4:31; Col. 3:8).

BITTERNESS, RESENTMENT

Resentment and bitterness are very closely related. One dictionary defines both as a feeling of deep anger and ill will. These very destructive feelings develop if we nurse our anger. Hebrews 12:15 tells us, "See to it that...no root of bitterness springing up causes trouble."

Anger has the potential to move us to all of these responses. These are all examples of the perversion of our anger, which now moves us away from God and toward evil and destructive acts and attitudes. It is because of these responses that anger gets its reputation as a "deadly sin." But notice that responding to anger in these ways gives us no help in understanding the "primary pain" that stimulated our anger in the first place. They do not help us answer God's question to Cain: "Why are you angry?"

ASSERTIVENESS

Dr. Warren mentions assertiveness as a positive response to anger. I have omitted it from the diagram but mention it as one possible outcome of a conversation with Jesus. Assertiveness is an action, usually speech, that presents a case for one's desires, needs, or points of view. It is an important topic in itself, but we cannot pursue it here.

For our purposes, what is important is not confusing assertiveness with aggression. Some students in the courses I have taught have experienced this confusion. To learn more about assertiveness, I suggest you read about habit number four in Stephen Covey's book *The 7 Habits of Highly Effective People.* Assertiveness is the second part of the habit "Seek first to understand and then be understood."[7]

A CONVERSATION WITH JESUS

My contribution to this chart is the idea that anger can move us to have a conversation with Jesus. As we talk to Jesus about our anger, we can experience two possible outcomes. In most cases Jesus can show us how to defuse our anger and prevent destructive responses. In a few cases we can redirect our anger so it moves us to accomplish God's purposes in the world. We will describe these two outcomes more completely when we explore conversing with Jesus below.

This discipline of talking to Jesus about our anger actually goes back to the teachings of medieval theologians. For them anger management began with being patient and asking God to enlarge their hearts. Notice that they separated feelings of anger from its expression since they encouraged monks to pray when they felt angry. To learn this discipline, we need to become aware of and consciously weaken our old programmed responses to anger. If we can accomplish this, we will have won a major victory in being able to transform our emotions. What is happening is that our anger is now moving us *toward* God. This direction was God's original purpose for our emotions in creation.

OTHER ANSWERS TO THE QUESTION, "WHY ARE YOU ANGRY?"

"Primary pain" is a pretty vague concept. We can make progress in answering the question, "Why are you angry?" if we get more specific about the ways we can experience this primary pain. Looking at some of the sources of anger, described by American psychiatrists Les Carter and Frank Minirth, can help us. They have called anger "the emotion of self-preservation"[8] and identify three areas in our lives we are programmed to preserve.

PERSONAL WORTH—Responding to events that devalue us or show lack of respect

ESSENTIAL NEEDS—Responding when our essential needs are unmet or invalidated

BASIC CONVICTIONS—Responding with assertiveness rather than aggression when our values are attacked

PRESERVING PERSONAL WORTH

When an event occurs (circle one in Figure 5-1) that the appraisal system of our brains labels as lack of respect or devaluing, our personal worth is attacked. In most people the limbic system in our brains interprets this (circle two) as a situation in which we must fight back and stimulates anger (circle three). We then must choose a response (circle four). When this happens to us, which of the responses in Figure 5-2 do we choose?

Here the primary pain is an attack on our identity. Such an attack produces shame feelings, although we might not be aware of them. (Do you remember our discussion of shame in Chapter 3?) These painful shame feelings move us to anger.

But shame feelings can also make us want to hide. So instead of thinking of defending ourselves, we experience fear and withdraw emotionally from the situation. Thus, depending on our personality and social situation, an attack on our identity that would produce anger in many people produces fear instead. This is an example of sublimation, which we mentioned earlier.

I believe this sublimation pattern was established early in my life. That is the reason why I don't experience much anger. I experience fear instead.

Pause at this point and do the next Reflection Exercise. It is designed to help you explore a possible answer for why you are angry.

PRESERVING ESSENTIAL NEEDS

All of us have basic survival needs; we need food, shelter, and safety. But as human beings we have more complex needs. We have relationship needs for acceptance and love. We have needs for security and significance. We have needs for useful work and recreation. Situations that deprive people of these needs produce anger. Such anger produces the energy needed to fight to preserve these essential needs. For refugees or oppressed people, these deprivations can be a significant source of anger. Many of these people have been denied the essential needs of food, shelter, safety, and respect. As a consequence, huge reservoirs of anger can exist in these populations.

Applying "the preserving essential needs" clarification of primary pain can lead to problems in our affluent Western culture. Often we "redefine" things we *want* as essential needs. And when something happens that prevents us from obtaining what we want, we get angry. When we have a conversation with Jesus and when the answer to the question, "Why are you angry?" is, "I am angry because [fill in the blank] kept me from getting an essential need met," we must ask Jesus whether our "needs" are really our desires. Then we need to find out what Jesus wants us to do with our desires.

Did you ever listen to a political speech in which the speaker argued for something you believed was wrong? I remember listening to a news broadcast in which a lady argued against a bill to prevent partial-birth abortions because, she said, it violated the "mother's right to choose." A partial-birth abortion is a procedure used during the final stages of pregnancy, when birth is induced. Then, when the baby is partially born, he or she is killed in a disgusting way. Strong anger feelings rose up inside me because, in my view, this lady was defending a barbaric procedure and was completely unconscious of the fact that the life of an innocent child was being destroyed.

My basic convictions or values were being attacked, and my anger feelings ignited. It is only fair to point out, however, that if I had responded to my values in an aggressive way, I would have attacked this lady's basic conviction that a woman has the right to choose what happens to her body. In turn, this lady would have felt angry. You can see how this kind of situation has the potential of leading to a heated argument. These arguments can then escalate to the point that aggressive actions are taken. The murder in the United States of a doctor who performed abortions is an example of how anger in response to a violation of our basic convictions can lead to terrible actions.

Reflection Exercise

See if you can remember an experience when someone attacked or treated with disrespect one of your basic convictions. What emotional response did you have? What response did your emotions move you to take?

Anger that arises because of a threat to our basic convictions is a place where we need to distinguish assertiveness from aggression. As Christians, we need to have the courage and strength that anger provides to make a case for our beliefs, but we need to do so in an atmosphere of respect and even love for the other person. Anyone who has tried to respect or love someone who has attacked one of our basic convictions will recognize it is extremely difficult.

When you think about your own anger, do you still have trouble pinpointing the primary pain that stimulated it? Different authors have emphasized other things that can stimulate our anger. Some of these anger stimulants are injustice, control or domination, unmet expectations, abuse, and shame. Let's briefly examine each of these.

Injustice

I previously mentioned that Doctors Allender and Longman regard anger as primarily a response to injustice.[9] When we read the Old Testament, we find many examples of God's anger burning toward injustice.

> Now the Lord saw, and it was displeasing in His sight that there was no justice. And He saw that there was no man, and was astonished that there was no one to intercede; then His own arm brought salvation to Him, and His righteousness upheld Him. He put on righteousness like a breastplate, and a helmet of salvation on His head; and He put on garments of vengeance for clothing and wrapped Himself with zeal as a mantle. According to their deeds, so He will repay, wrath to His adversaries, recompense to His enemies; to the coastlands He will make recompense. So they will fear the name of the Lord from the west and His glory from the rising of the sun, for He will come like a rushing stream which the wind of the Lord drives. (Isa. 59:15b–18)

Here we have a picture of God as a mighty warrior, whose wrath is ignited by a lack of justice. Many passages in Scripture like this led Doctors Allender and Longman to make the statement quoted earlier and to link destroying sin with injustice. When a situation comes to us and the evaluation process in our minds determines it is unjust, we respond with anger. (See circles two and three in Figure 5-1.)

We can see this dynamic at work when we remember a time when we were angry. At this time, if we listened to what our minds said about the anger-producing situation, we would probably hear, *That wasn't fair.*

I believe that when Jesus healed the man with the withered hand on the Sabbath, injustice stimulated his anger. In this case a religious system that looked with contempt on handicapped people created the injustice. If we think deeply about all the sources of primary pain, I believe it is possible to trace all of them to a root of injustice.

Reflection Exercise

Find a quiet place and remember specific events in the past when you were angry. See if you can remember the thoughts that went through your mind at the time. How many times did you think, *That's not fair* or *That's unjust?*

CONTROL OR DOMINATION

Does it ever seem like people and circumstances deprive you of your God-given privilege to choose for yourself? Feeling imprisoned by a controlling environment can stimulate anger. A situation where there is control and domination over you gives rise to a feeling of helplessness. Often in such situations all three areas discussed under self-preservation are threatened. So, for many people, experiences of control and domination might be the best way to describe their primary pain.

God never intended for others and circumstances to control us. He has given us a will to choose. Choosing his will is his best for us, but he never coerces us. He gives us freedom. Thus, anger in these circumstances can be a stimulus to move us to exercise the freedom he has given us.

Reflection Exercise

God has made each of us unique. Have you ever been in situations where you didn't believe you could be yourself? Where you had to conform to the expectations or demands of others? What feelings were you having during those situations? Often we might answer, "I feel like rebelling." What do you think might be an underlying feeling to the desire to rebel?

Unmet Expectations

From the time we get up in the morning, we have expectations of what our day will be like. Often when these expectations are unmet, we find ourselves feeling angry. We may call this form of anger "frustration." Our own experience can be our instructor in this area. Remember a situation you went into with certain expectations. It could be going to a class, entering into a relationship, beginning a new job, or going on a vacation. What happened to your emotions when your expectations were unmet? Some possible names for your feelings during such a situation could be "angry," "irritated," or "frustrated."

If we listen to our self-talk, we often find our minds saying, *That was unfair.* The evaluation process in our brains (circle number two in Figure 5-1) links unmet expectations with injustice, and we experience anger. Pondering our discussion so far, you may also find that your evaluation system links unmet expectations to beliefs that our essential needs are unmet or that our personal worth is threatened. We discover, however, that unmet expectations are the best ways to describe the anger that leads to conflict in marriage, in ministry teams, or in work situations.

Abuse

"Personal attacks," "boundary violations," and "hurts" are other names we can give to areas we covered under self-preservation. In your conversation with God, maybe these names are more helpful than thinking in terms of personal worth, essential needs, or basic convictions. It is important to note that all forms of abuse fall into this category and have the potential to stimulate anger.

Shame

We previously discussed the link between feelings of shame and anger. Since anger gives us a sense of power, while shame makes us feel small and weak, expressions of anger counteract these shame feelings.

Processing Anger by Conversing with Jesus

We have come to the point where we have a number of possible answers to the question, "Why are you angry?" in our conversation with Jesus. Now

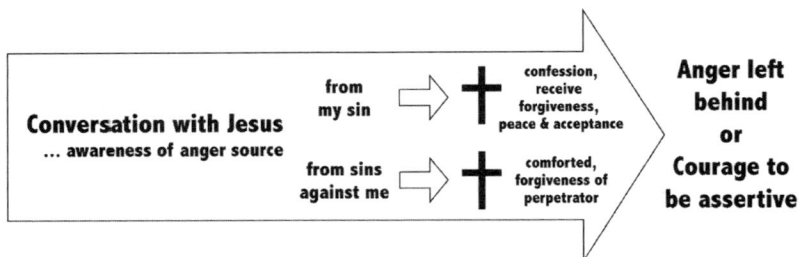

Figure 5-3

we need to go to the second challenge—talking to Jesus about what to do with our anger. Let's look at Figure 5-3 to see where the conversation goes from here.

Our basic plan in all our conversations with Jesus about emotions is to maintain a sense of his presence with us and allow him to lead us to the cross. At the cross Jesus accomplished all his redemptive work. At the cross we can receive revelation of how Jesus sees the situation that precipitated our anger.

Let's review some of the things God accomplished when Jesus died on the cross. At the cross Jesus took the sins of all people onto himself. The result is that for those who put their faith in Jesus, an exchange takes place. Jesus bore our sins on the cross and in exchange gives us his righteousness. "He made Him who knew no sin to be sin on our behalf, so that we might become the righteousness of God in Him" (2 Cor. 5:21). How this works is a mystery worked out in the council of the Trinity before the world was made (see Eph. 1:4–5, 9).

In our conversations with Jesus, we consider first how we work with our own unrighteous anger. When our anger moves us to a destructive act against someone else, we sin against that person, and we sin against God, because in these acts we do not reflect his image. Often this kind of anger comes about because we have unrealistic expectations of the other person. It may also arise because our selfish desires, programmed into us because of the fall, make unreasonable demands on others, which they are unable to meet. When we find ourselves with any of the negative responses to anger pictured in Figure 5-2, we need to talk with Jesus about these negative actions and attitudes. Our process is depicted in the upper portion of Figure 5–3.

We first need revelation from Jesus about the nature of our sin. When God asked Cain why he was angry, he may have wanted Cain to get in touch with the envy or hatred he had toward his brother. To be willing to face our sins brings the painful emotion of shame and requires God's grace and strength to do so. When we face our guilt and realize we have failed in our God-given task to be his image, we take the next step and confess our sins. First John 1:9 says, "If we confess our sins, He is faithful and righteous to forgive us our sins and to cleanse us from all unrighteousness." The Greek word translated *confess* in this passage means "to agree with." Our conversation with Jesus brings us to the place where we can agree with him that our act or attitude was sinful. We can then experience the result of the exchange that took place on the cross. We can know that we are accepted in the family of God and again experience the peace of Christ ruling in our hearts. When this happens, we find that our anger has disappeared.

But Jesus died not only for our sins but for the sins of those *who have sinned against us*. As we have our conversation with Jesus, we need to remember that the sins of another person against us were included in the redemption Jesus accomplished on the cross. As our High Priest, he is able to release us from the emotional and spiritual bondage those sins produced. This lifting of the consequences of others' sins against us takes place as we release to Jesus our need for justice in regard to those who have sinned against us, and as we ask for grace to forgive them. If we can receive grace to forgive those who have sinned against us, then we no longer need our anger. We can leave it at the foot of the cross. This truth is depicted in the lower portion of Figure 5-3.

But forgiving those who have wounded us and releasing our desire for justice to Jesus aren't easy steps. They can be especially difficult when emotional wounds are very deep. Before we can enter into the process of forgiveness, we need comfort from Jesus. We need to hear from him about how he wants to use the wounding situation for his purposes in our lives. In many cases this wounding will result in a struggle with our beliefs about God's character and about how he works in our lives. The lower section of Figure 5-3 summarizes the events that need to take place in our conversation with Jesus.

As we mentioned above, our first need is comfort. Isaiah 53:4 says, "Surely our griefs He Himself bore, and our sorrows He carried; yet we ourselves esteemed Him stricken, smitten of God, and afflicted." Jesus carried our griefs, the sadness associated with our losses, and our emotional pains on the cross. Paul told us in 2 Corinthians 1:3–5 that our God is now a God of comfort. "Blessed be the God and Father of our Lord Jesus Christ, the Father of mercies and God of all comfort, who comforts us in all our affliction so that we will be able to comfort those who are in any affliction with the comfort with which we ourselves are comforted by God. For just as the sufferings of Christ are ours in abundance, so also our comfort is abundant through Christ."

In our interaction with Jesus, we need to ask him to bring God's comfort to our pain. This part of the process may not be completed in a single conversation with Jesus. We may have to have a number of different conversations with God about this pain. We may also need to seek out a wise brother or sister or counselor in the Lord, asking the person to come alongside us and help us receive God's comfort for this pain in our souls.

The important point is that as we begin to receive God's comfort, we can relinquish our anger to Jesus on the cross and ask him for directions about what to do next. Most of the time he will respond, "Let me have your anger and let my compassion and commitment to justice deal with the persons who have sinned against you." In a few cases he might respond, "I want you to keep some of your anger because it will give you the emotional strength and courage to address the unjust situation." But in both cases, our forgiveness frees us from the burdens of bitterness and desires for revenge, enabling us to live in love for the offending person. We are no longer victims. We are free to pursue the abundant life Jesus wants to give us.

We must realize that this whole process of facing the pain that stimulates our anger, being able to identify and name that pain, bringing it to Jesus on the cross, receiving comfort, and forgiving and releasing those who have wounded us may take some time. Often we lack the capacity to face all the pain in our initial conversation with Jesus. So we need to be willing to process our pain in steps. This is another place where a wise counselor or spiritual friend who understands these things can be helpful.[10]

When anger functions to move us to work with the pain in our lives, and when, in the process, we draw closer to Jesus, we can see one of the redemptive purposes God has for anger. In this case we can agree with Dr. Warren that "anger is a gift of God." Our anger has moved us to identify the pain in our hearts and draws us closer to Jesus to experience healing for this pain.

ADDITIONAL COMMENTS ABOUT INJUSTICE

Our brains are programmed to respond to perceived injustice with anger. It is tempting to conclude that when injustice is responsible for our anger, our anger is justified and that we should act on it, but we need to exercise caution here.

First, we need to ask whether the injustice was directed at us or at someone else. In the examples we have in the Gospels of Jesus being angry, his anger was always directed at those responsible for injustice toward others. During all the events surrounding the crucifixion, when the injustice was directed at him, we do not see him expressing anger. When injustice is directed at us, we need to follow the procedure described about conversing with Jesus when we have been sinned against to know how to respond to our anger feelings.

When in our conversation with Jesus he asks us to keep some of our anger to confront an unjust situation directed at us, we must meet the forgiveness condition before we take such action. Dr. Allender gives an example of such a confrontation.[11]

When the injustice is directed at others, we need to talk with Jesus about what action he wants us to take. Anger arising in these situations has led many to get involved in efforts to free people from slavery or sexual exploitation. It can also be a strong motivation to pray for the oppressed in the world wherever they are.

OTHER STIMULANTS FOR ANGER: UNMET EXPECTATIONS

When we desire something to take place in the future and events or people stand in the way of achieving our hopes, our brains respond with anger.[12] In our lives we often have expectations based on our cultural and family experiences. We carry these expectations with us in our interactions with family, work, and other life situations. Sometimes when people don't respond according to our expectations, our anger is stimulated. Sometimes we interpret these events as unjust or unfair. So anger from this cause gets confused with anger at injustice.

In our conversation with Jesus, when unmet expectations are the source of our anger, we need revelation about our expectations. Are they realistic? Are they expressions of our selfish desires? One of the things we may discover is that an unmet expectation is a situation where we have experienced a loss. The appropriate emotion for loss is sadness, not anger (we will talk about dealing with sadness in the next chapter). In our conversation, Jesus may tell us to learn about "speaking the truth in love" (Eph. 4:15). In this case we need to learn how to be assertive to make our desires known. Or Jesus may tell us to overlook the matter. We will expand on this response in the next section.

LETTING GO OF ANGER

In many situations where we converse with Jesus about our anger, he may respond with the message of Proverbs 19:11. "A man's discretion makes him slow to anger, and it is his glory to overlook a transgression." Paul picked up this theme in Colossians 3:13. "Bearing with one another, and forgiving each other, whoever has a complaint against anyone; just as the Lord forgave you, so also should you." This statement follows his injunction to us to "put on a heart of compassion, kindness, humility, gentleness and patience" (v. 12). To reflect the image of God in the midst of the surroundings where he has placed us, we need to model kindness, gentleness, and patience with those around us. This is especially powerful when we model these attributes to those who annoy us in some way. Learning to let go of our anger is a practical way to make the presence of Jesus known in our relationships.

A final part of our conversations with Jesus is to thank him for his love and care for us and for the insights we have received. It is good to have a time of worship and to end our conversation with a request for the Holy Spirit to continue to remind us to use the experience of anger to *move* us to enter into a conversation with Jesus *before* we respond to our anger. In this way we will process our anger before the sun sets and prevent it from becoming a deadly sin (Eph. 4:26–27). We will have made further progress in training our elephants to respond as the new people we have become in Jesus.

In the next chapter we explore sadness, but we will also discover that we are not finished with anger. As we explore responses to sadness, using the skills presented in this chapter will help us when anger rises again.

Six

FROM SADNESS TO COMFORT

"Blessed are those who mourn, for they shall be comforted."
MATTHEW 5:4

"Blessed be the God and Father of our Lord Jesus Christ, the Father of mercies and God of all comfort, who comforts us in all our affliction so that we will be able to comfort those who are in any affliction with the comfort with which we ourselves are comforted by God. For just as the sufferings of Christ are ours in abundance, so also our comfort is abundant through Christ."

2 CORINTHIANS 1:3–5

When I was four years old, my father brought home some baby chicks, and we kept them in a box in our kitchen. I really enjoyed watching those tiny birds dance around in their box. I especially liked to hold and pet them. They were so fluffy and cuddly.

For reasons we never discovered, the chicks began to die. Finally, only one was left. My mother helped me put a mirror in the box so the remaining chick wouldn't think it was alone. She told me, "We don't want the chick to die of loneliness." This touched something in my little-child heart. I was an only child and had spent much time alone.

One day the last chick died. I experienced a deep, profound sadness. I must not have been able to process that experience well because even now, at age eighty, I respond with tears when I relate this story. My sadness brought me the message: *You have lost something.*

Loss is a constant companion in life. All of us are aware of loss when a relative or close friend dies, but we may not be aware of the many losses that regularly beset us during the course of our lives. Loss of praise from a superior at work, loss of energy due to aging, the failure to achieve a goal—these are all losses that may escape our immediate awareness. On the other hand, we also experience losses we are all too aware of: the loss of health, an unfulfilled expectation, the loss of a job, or the dissolution of a marriage. Sadness is the emotional signal that comes to us when those losses occur.

The Language Surrounding Sadness and Loss

I would like to spend a little time sorting through the words we use in connection with sadness and loss, beginning with the words *grief* and *sadness*. Sometimes these two words are used interchangeably, but I would like to make a distinction. I want to use *sadness* to represent the core emotion that comes with loss. When my baby chick died, the emotion I experienced was sadness. I cried when I found out the chick was no more.

I use *grief* to describe the process of experiencing that emotion over time. For a number of weeks after the chick died, I woke up at night and again felt the sadness. But then I began to process what had happened. Why had the chick died? Could I have done something to prevent its death? During those times, I experienced grief. Grief can involve many emotions. We will discuss some of them later.

Mourning is a word that describes the outer and inner activities we go through as we respond to loss. Grieving and mourning are closely related and often used interchangeably. As the verses at the beginning of this chapter point out, God's design for us is to mourn. Because our God is a God of comfort, his goal is that mourning will lead us to experience his comfort. But the journey from loss to comfort is rarely a short or easy one. Learning how to take this journey is part of learning how to reflect the image of God in the circumstances where he has placed us.

Though the journey from loss to comfort is different for each person, it usually involves three tasks:

1. We must allow ourselves to acknowledge our loss and feel the sadness that accompanies it.
2. We must learn how to mourn. That means we must understand the grieving process and how to participate in it.

3. We must learn how to receive comfort from God.

Let's explore these three tasks in more detail.

ALLOWING OURSELVES TO ACKNOWLEDGE OUR LOSS AND EXPERIENCE SADNESS

In our modern globalized culture, we live in a milieu that focuses on youth, pleasure, and personal fulfillment. Many view loss, sadness, and mourning as intruders to be dispensed with as quickly and easily as possible. For this reason we have learned to minimize any sense of loss and deny our feelings of sadness.

Consequently we cannot move on to the second task—mourning. This is especially true for men. Society teaches men from the beginning of their lives not to cry. They receive the message "Life is tough. To be a man, you need to be tough." For most men, to talk about one's feelings is a sign of weakness. This is changing some in modern times, but men still carry a lot of this social programming. Women are more in touch with their feelings and are better able to talk about them, but many women share with men the lack of understanding about mourning and receiving comfort in response to sadness. The result is that much of our grief remains "underground." Instead of experiencing sadness and letting that lead us into mourning, we plunge into activity or pleasures that distract us from the pain of our loss.

Let me share a little of how grief worked in my life. I'm an only child. When I was in my late forties, I had the responsibility of dealing with the deaths of my aunt (who had no children), my mother, and my father—all within a three-year period. At the time I was a professor of chemistry in a large state university and had a family with three children. As I responded to these losses, I can recall how I went into what I call my "planning and action mode." I worked out all the details of the funerals, burials, and estate matters with scientific precision. I was completely out of touch with my feelings, except for a few minutes at the memorial service for my father. My plunge into activity successfully kept me from feeling the pain of my losses.

Three years later, when I found myself with nothing to do for a few hours, out of nowhere I experienced a deep feeling of sadness about the loss of my father. I found a place where I could be undisturbed and wept for about an hour. As I wept, some of my unfulfilled dreams about doing things with my dad flooded through my mind. One of these was for the two of us to go on a fishing trip together. My dad became paralyzed during the last few years of his life, and I was never able to work out how to do the trip.

After a while I found myself praying for my dad, even though he was dead, and asking God to comfort him for all the losses he had experienced in his life. As I was praying in this way, I began to feel a deep sense of love for him. While I was experiencing all these thoughts and emotions, I found myself feeling comforted as well. I realized much later that comfort came while I was having a conversation with God about my losses.

There was nothing in my growing-up years that prepared me for this kind of experience. There was nothing that had taught me how to mourn. This time of experiencing sadness and weeping over the loss of my father began a journey of learning how to acknowledge my losses and to make proper use of the feeling of sadness.

In your life you will also be tempted to deny sadness and loss. To help you to stop running away from feelings of sadness and to listen to the message these feelings are trying to bring, I invite you to do the next Reflection Exercise.

Reflection Exercise

Think back over the last few months and write down at least two losses in your life. They don't need to be major events like deaths. They can be failure to fulfill a dream, the departure of a friend, a loss of health, or the loss of a sense of well-being. For each of these losses, try to remember what happened when you first became aware of them. What feelings did you have? What did you tell yourself? What did you do? Did you try to escape the sad feeling through activity or some kind of pleasure?

LOSS AND ADDICTIONS

Activity isn't the only thing that keeps us from allowing ourselves to feel sadness during a time of loss. We can distract ourselves with anything that gives us pleasure. Alcohol, drugs, extreme sports, shopping, eating, sex, and

Internet porn all provide pleasurable distractions that keep us from experiencing the pain of our loss. But the problem with these pleasures is twofold.

First, the relief we experience is only temporary. Second, all pleasures are subject to adaptation or habituation. This means that the more frequently we participate in a pleasure, the less pleasurable it becomes. This is a neurological fact of life.

We find only two ways to get around adaptation. One way is to discipline ourselves to space our pleasures. Let me illustrate. I love Swiss chocolate. When my wife and I travel to Switzerland, we always bring back several packages. To keep from experiencing adaptation, I must be careful to let time elapse between eating portions of the chocolate. If I ate a whole package at once, the last bite would no longer be pleasurable. So a Swiss chocolate bar lasts me a month.

When we use pleasure to escape pain, however, spacing our pleasures doesn't seem attractive. The second way is to intensify the pleasure in some way. Choosing this way puts us on a path to addiction. The easy availability and various intensity levels of Internet porn, for example, make this an easy, attractive way for men to escape the pain of loss.[1]

LOSS AND SIN

In preceding chapters we outlined the role of sin in the emotions of shame and anger. Sin is also an important source of our losses. We need to make the same distinctions we made earlier and examine sin from two vantage points: our own sins and the sins of others against us. Since we looked at sin from these two vantage points in earlier chapters, we will only talk about some of their unique applications to sadness.

Our sin inevitably leads to some kind of loss, both to ourselves and to others. Our unprocessed anger, which turns to resentment, leads to broken relationships. Unfaithfulness can lead to the loss of a marriage. When we let denial move us into an addiction, we can lose many things—our jobs, our health, our relationships. We didn't talk about this in Chapter 5, but much of the primary pain stimulating our anger comes from unprocessed losses. So our inability to process our sadness often leaves us in the anger stage of the grief process. If we do not know how to process our anger, it manifests its reputation as one of the seven deadly sins.

The sins of others against us produce loss. All abuse produces some kind of loss. Only as we gain insight into the extent and nature of these losses can we receive comfort from God and receive grace to forgive those who have sinned against us.

We will expand on these thoughts later when we talk about entering into a conversation with Jesus about sadness.

UNDERSTANDING THE GRIEVING PROCESS

The second task we mentioned above was to understand the grieving process and learn how to mourn. Most treatments of the grieving process are built on the foundation of Elizabeth Kubler-Ross's study on dying patients. She described five stages people pass through when they face a loss.

1. Denial
2. Depression
3. Anger
4. Bargaining
5. Acceptance [2]

Everyone responds to loss differently, so realizing that not necessarily everyone experiences these stages in the above order is important. In addition, people can experience more than one stage at a time, then go back and forth between different stages. In some cases they can skip one or more stages. Grieving or mourning is the process of getting through these various stages and reaching what Kubler-Ross and others call acceptance. The thesis of this chapter is that the Bible describes this last stage as comfort.

DENIAL

We already treated denial in our discussion of the first task in our journey from loss to comfort. To start the grieving process, we need to find a way out of denial. For non-Christians, often only a crisis, a "hitting bottom," a sense of hopeless despair, can bring people out of denial. Non-Christian scientists argue that the human brain is programmed to envision a future that can surmount the despair in the present. They argue that this is the basis for the distinctly human characteristic of hope. [3] But there is no discussion of how the transition out of denial and into hope takes place.

For Christians, coming out of denial is also difficult. But we have two additional resources that can help us before we have to go through a hitting-bottom crisis. One resource is that we are encouraged to develop spiritual friends. [4] A spiritual friend is someone we trust who can lovingly challenge us to examine our lives.

The second resource Christians have is the discipline of conversing with Jesus about our emotions when we sense things are wrong in our lives. In situations where denial might be a problem, Jesus can open the eyes of our hearts—so we can see how we've been living in denial—and lead us on in our journey of grief. Then we must discipline ourselves to resist the temptation to go back into denial. Our goals are to embrace and even welcome feelings of sadness.

DEPRESSION

One common way people respond to loss is depression. We are left with a feeling of emptiness and loss of motivation. Life has lost its zest. No activity seems worthwhile. This form of depression is called "reactive depression" because it is a reaction to losses in our lives. We should distinguish reactive depression from "endogenous depression," which is linked to our genetics and involves abnormalities in our brain chemistry.

I experienced reactive depression a few years ago because of a crisis in my family. My youngest son was convicted of a crime and had to pay the legal consequences. This event sent shock waves rippling through my whole family. My picture of our family as a loving and connected one was shattered.

For several months I felt empty inside. I lost motivation. I experienced all the symptoms of reactive depression. During this time I had many opportunities to apply the teachings of this chapter by inviting Jesus into my emptiness and asking him to help me experience anew a sense that he was present and still working to glorify himself in my family. As the consequences of my son's actions drag on, I have to continue to fight the battle against depression that comes upon me as new dimensions of my loss are revealed. During this depression phase, Jesus has enabled me, through my conversations with him, to name and process my losses more fully. [5]

As we get in touch with the dimensions of our loss, we may next become angry. (As you did the Reflection Exercise earlier in this chapter, was anger one of your emotions?) To the extent that something deep within us believes the loss was unjust or unfair, our feeling of anger makes sense (see Chapter 5). "Why" questions often accompany this feeling of anger. Why did my friend have to leave me? Why did I have to get sick? Why did God let this happen to me?

Usually "why" questions like these are not really questions. That is, we know somewhere within us there are no answers to them. These questions express our frustrations or feelings of helplessness. The challenge is to learn to use the anger and frustration we feel to move us to clarify the full extent of the loss—to explore it and talk about it. As we explore our loss in a conversation with Jesus, we gain insight into his perception and goals for our lives, and he can convert our anger into sadness. Sadness is an emotion that can lead to mourning, which can lead to comfort. Sadness moves us along in the grief process, but anger keeps us stuck with nowhere to go.

Dr. Archibald Hart argues that anger and resentment can be a mask for male depression. [6] Here we see a linkage between several stages of the grief process. Loss, depression, and anger can all be tied together. We often need a wise counselor or spiritual friend to help us untangle these issues.

One way we can transform our anger over loss into something productive is to have a deeper understanding of suffering. Here Christians have an advantage over nonbelievers. We Christians understand that we live in a world that isn't functioning correctly. Romans 8:22–23 says, "For we know that the whole creation groans and suffers the pains of childbirth together until now. And not only this, but also we ourselves, having the first fruits of the Spirit, even we ourselves groan within ourselves, waiting eagerly for our adoption as sons, the redemption of our body."

Our losses remind us that sin has infected our world and that the whole creation groans over the fact that God's will is not yet being done on earth as it is in heaven. So we can ask the Holy Spirit to use our anger and "why" questions to move us to cry out to God to hasten the day when Jesus will return. Then we will experience our adoption as sons and the redemption of our bodies.

It isn't fair when young people die of leukemia or babies are born with birth defects, but our faith in a loving and sovereign God cries out to him with our frustration over these things, asking him to come. So even our anger and "why" questions can move us to relate to God in a more intimate way. Out of this intimate relationship, God may reveal to us new ways he wants us to participate in the alleviation of suffering. These verses, along with many others, form the basis of Christian hope. We will say more about hope and suffering in the next chapter about joy.

BARGAINING

Some people experience a bargaining stage in their grief process. Christians may be tempted to participate in this part of the grief process. "God, if you will heal my body from this disease, I will serve you more fervently." "Lord, if you help me make my mortgage payment and keep my house, I will tithe." While Christians may try to bargain with God, non-Christians may bargain with life.

Bargaining doesn't help us reach the acceptance or comfort stage of our grief. At the root of bargaining is the idea that somehow the loss came about because of something we did or didn't do. We bargain out of a false assumption, of which we may be unaware, that if we could have done things differently, the loss wouldn't have occurred. Bargaining may be indicative of a belief that losses occur because we have sinned. There may be cases where our loss is the direct result of our sin. In those cases, instead of bargain, we need to repent and confess our sin. Repentance and confession open the door to experience God's grace and mercy. Bargaining puts us in the place of trying to manipulate God by our efforts. This can never lead to comfort.

ACCEPTANCE AND COMFORT

The goal of the grief process is to receive God's comfort, to know that in our loss we participate in the "groans" (Rom. 8:22) of the universe until the day when God sets things right, to know that God's promise is that our "momentary, light affliction is producing for us an eternal weight of glory" (2 Cor. 4:17). Non-Christians call this stage "acceptance." Acceptance means we reach a place where we realize that, in spite of our loss, we can still survive and—to some extent—live a meaningful life. Acceptance puts the loss in perspective.

Christians have something more powerful than acceptance. We can experience the comfort of a loving and sovereign God, who isn't aloof to our suffering but entered into it as Jesus. Jesus suffered all the consequences of sin in this world so we might be accepted into the family of God and might experience the hope of sharing his glory. Our God calls himself the "God of all comfort" (2 Cor. 1:3).

SADNESS AND REJECTION

One feeling we often talk about is rejection. Have you ever asked yourself, *What am I feeling when I say I am feeling rejected?* The question is complex because in one sense rejection isn't really a feeling. It's a belief deep in our hearts that we've been rejected. Strong feelings surround this belief; that is why we say we "feel" rejected.

When I was giving a seminar in Korea, one student asked about the feelings of rejection he had experienced because his father left home. He had missed out on all the things God designed fathers to give to their sons. As I pondered how to answer that question, the thought came to me: *Those things are really losses, and the appropriate feeling is that of sadness.* Many events that lead to our sense of rejection are really losses. We need revelation to be able to name these losses, grieve over them, and receive the Lord's comfort for them.

For example, it *is* a loss when no father is present to help his son learn how to hit a baseball or ride a bike. Because the son might not have learned these development skills at an appropriate time, due to his father's absence, he might be left out of neighborhood games or activities. In this way his "belief" that his father rejected him is tied to his unnamed feelings of sadness, which his loss is trying to produce.

In Chapter 3 we talked about how feelings of shame can also be tied to beliefs about rejection. So one of the things that happens as we learn to converse with Jesus about rejection is that these links between our beliefs and emotions can be untangled. Jesus can then bring comfort to heal our sadness and a new identity to heal our shame. We can leave our rejection at the foot of the cross.

Type A and Type B Traumas

Some trauma counselors find it convenient to divide traumas into two types.[7] Type A traumas are those we experience because of the absence of something that would be "normal" for us to receive. In the example above, the young boy experienced a Type A trauma because of his father's absence and the absence of things a father provides for his son. Type B traumas are those we experience because something bad has happened to us. All abuse brings Type B traumas.

Type A traumas are more difficult to deal with than Type B traumas, because we don't often recognize them as traumas. They seem to be a normal part of living, but both types of trauma produce losses. And all these losses will have consequences in our lives if we do not process them. Learning how to converse with Jesus about our shame, anger, depression, and sadness can help us gain insight into the nature of these traumas and how they may still influence our emotional lives in the present.

A Model Conversation with Jesus about Sadness and Loss

The journey from loss to comfort is such an individual experience that describing how a conversation with Jesus about sadness and loss should look is difficult. In previous chapters, we have learned the basics of how to converse with Jesus about an emotional experience. In this chapter I present a model conversation with God that outlines some of the ways a conversation about sadness and loss might proceed.

I have left blanks so you can fill in your personal responses. The important thing is that you try it out so you can learn how this model might work for you. Remember to establish a relational connection with Jesus before diving into the painful feelings of sadness. You want to take Jesus with you throughout the whole conversation. If you find that you have lost the sense of his presence, go back to the interactive or appreciation memory chairs until you can sense his presence with you again.

> Thank you, Lord, that you wept when your friend Lazarus died, that you wept over Jerusalem. When Isaiah prophesied about you, he called you a "man of sorrows and acquainted with grief" (53:3).

I thank you that you want to be with me when I am suffering from sorrow and grief. So I come to you now and ask you to help me understand and work through my sadness.

Lord, help me to identify my losses. Help me to name them and describe them as well as the effects they have had in my life. [Pause here and let the Lord respond to these requests. As you describe the effects of the losses, let yourself feel the emotions that come. Write down as many of these thoughts and feelings as you can.]

[If you feel angry, you might continue this way.] Lord, that loss [Describe it.] was very painful to me, and I'm angry. "Why" questions rise up within me. Why did this happen to me? Look at all the effects this has had in my life! [List them.] Lord, I realize that while I'm angry, I can't grieve. I want to fight. I want some kind of justice. I want to scream, "It's not fair!" But I realize the primary feeling I need is sadness. I need to weep. I need to accept the fact that these things are lost. Help me. Transform my anger into sadness and help me to mourn.

Use my anger to help me see that I'm participating in the suffering of a creation that is groaning in travail and waiting for the revelation of the sons of God. May my anger motivate me to cry out to you to hasten that day when Jesus will return and set things right. Lord, are there ways you want to use my anger to motivate me to enter into the battle against injustice? Show me practically how you want me to proceed with this.

Lord, some of my losses are the direct result of my sin. [Ask the Lord to show you if and how this is the case.] In this case, I want to confess to you my sin, turn from it, and ask you to cleanse me from all unrighteousness. But Lord, you have promised to be with me and to forgive me for my sins, and I want to ask you to be with me and strengthen me to take full responsibility for the consequences of my sinful actions. Give me grace to endure the pain of these losses. Please show me if there are people I need to make restitution to because they have suffered loss as the result of my sin.

Lord, I also realize that some of my losses have come about because I have been sinned against. Help me to name the ways I have been sinned against and bring those sins to the cross. Help me to confess the sins of others against me there and ask you to forgive those sins. Then, Lord, I ask you to lift the consequences of those sins from me. Come and comfort me. Lord, give me grace to forgive those who have sinned against me. [If you need further help in this area, review the sections in the shame and anger chapters, where we discussed this situation.]

Lord, as I let myself feel my sadness in your presence, I ask you to comfort me. Thank you for your Word that says, "Blessed are those who mourn for they shall be comforted" (Matt. 5:4). I thank you, Lord, that you are the "God of all comfort." I thank you for your promises that you will turn my mourning into dancing. I don't feel like dancing right now, but I want to believe and experience that promise.

Lord, I realize that mourning is a process. Help me to stay with you in this process until I receive the fullness of your comfort. When the time is right, give me feelings of sadness and help me to remember to let these feelings move me to have a further conversation with you. If feelings of sadness come when I can't mourn, remind me to quickly give these feelings to you and ask you to keep them for me and bring them back to me when we can talk about them together.

Thank you, Lord, that as I process these things with you, I feel closer to you, and our relationship becomes more intimate. Thank you, Lord, that you are glorified when my losses are filled with your comfort.

Mourning and Forgiveness

In the chapters about shame and anger, we discussed forgiving those who have sinned against us. You might want to review those sections, because the same considerations apply when praying about losses that are the result of others' sins against us. A modern author, writing about forgiveness, has said, "What cannot be successfully mourned remains like an indigestible lump in the psyche, a place of unbearable, irreparable loss that mars the self." [8] This author doesn't use a biblical approach but points out that forgiveness is an important measure of emotional development. To reach the goal of acceptance or comfort, it is necessary for forgiveness to come into play. That is the reason why even secular scientists argue that forgiveness is a necessary step to living a life in which we can flourish. [9]

Writing a Lamentation Psalm

One of the places where we can look to help us learn to mourn is the book of Psalms. Some of these psalms are called "lamentation psalms," because in them the author lists losses that have been suffered and the overwhelming feelings that go along with them. Also the Old Testament book of Lamentations is a weeping and lamenting over the fall of Jerusalem and the destruction of the temple. These were tremendous losses for the Jewish people. In addition, the whole book of Job is an example of Job's lamenting to God about losses that seemed unjust to him.

One can use these psalms of lament as a model to help us mourn our losses. For example, read through Psalms 44 and 55. One can find the following components in these and other psalms:

1. A recounting of past mercies (Ps. 44:1–3)
2. A description of present complaints (Ps. 44:9–16; 55:1–8)
3. A cry to God for deliverance (Ps. 44:23–26; 55:16–19)
4. An expression of trust in God (Ps. 44:4–8; 55:22)
5. A time of worship (Ps. 43:3–4)

One practical step I have found to be helpful is writing my own lamentation psalm. To do this, I write out my own expression of each of the components above. I encourage you to do the same in the following exercise.

Reflection Exercise

Take a situation in which you feel angry, sad, or both about a loss in your life. Write out a lamentation psalm, using the components above as an outline. Describe your complaint in as much detail as possible. This is a place where you can express your anger about the situation. Use some of the complaints you find in the book of Psalms to help you. After you write out your psalm, you may want to read it aloud with feeling to the Lord or a trusted friend. That was what the psalmist did. After doing so, write down in your personal journal the effects this exercise had on your life

God has designed us for another emotion that can counteract all the negative feelings and beliefs that come to us through shame, fear, anger, and sadness. That is the emotion of joy, the subject of the next chapter.

SEVEN

EXPERIENCING JOY

In Your presence is fullness of joy.

PSALM 16:11

And the ransomed of the Lord will return and come with joyful shouting to Zion, with everlasting joy upon their heads. They will find gladness and joy, and sorrow and sighing will flee away.

ISAIAH 35:10

While I was working as a professor of chemistry, I traveled to scientific meetings. In those days one could go to the concourse to meet arriving passengers as they exited the airplane. My wife, Sarah, would come to pick me up at the airport.

I remember the anticipation I felt as I walked down the exit ramp, straining my neck to see if I could catch sight of Sarah as she waited in the arrival area. When our eyes made contact and I saw the sudden smile as she recognized me, I experienced a surge of ecstatic emotion. I didn't have a name for this emotion then. Later, I discovered I was experiencing joy.

As we study more about God's design for the world he has made, we find that at the core of spiritual reality are three characteristics that have strong emotional components. They are love, joy, and peace.

Love includes feelings of compassion. Joy produces feelings of delight, wonder, and well-being. Peace brings feelings of tranquility and contentment. These three emotions are first in the list of the "fruit of the Spirit" given in Galatians 5:22. All three are major themes in the New Testament. Of these three facets of human experience, joy is the only one that is purely emotional. Recall that the capacity for joy is one of the core emotions built into our brains from birth. A newborn baby experiences joy. Love and peace are emotions that come about only as we develop language and the ability to interact reflectively with other people and our environment.

In previous chapters we focused on what many often refer to as "negative emotions." Their negative reputation comes about because they bring unpleasant or painful feelings, and sometimes they move us to destructive consequences. The theme of this book is that when we process these "negative" emotions by inviting Jesus into them and conversing with him about them, he transforms them so we experience a positive outcome. Do you remember the story of the caregiver in Chapter 3? She brought the infant back to "joy camp" after an emotionally painful event. In this chapter I want to show that Jesus can be like this wise caregiver and can bring us back to joy, even when we have suffered a painful event.

Situations Where We Find Joy

A common place where we discover joy is when a reunion occurs after a separation. My story about meeting Sarah at the airport after a separation is an example. Do you remember seeing pictures of the Chilean miners after they were trapped in a mine and then reunited with their families? Much joy was present. One sees the same joy when military families are reunited after a spouse was deployed overseas. Notice in these examples that joy is present because of the pain of separation.

We find similar joy-producing situations in Luke 15, where Jesus told three stories. In each story, something is lost and then found. We find a bringing together of things that belonged together but had been separated. The proper relationship between the elements in the story is restored.

The first story is about a lost sheep. The second is about lost coins. The third is about a lost son. In each story, when the lost person or item was found, that which had been lost was reunited to the place where it belonged. This was an occasion for celebration. Great joy characterized these celebrations.

Jesus told all three stories to illustrate the point that great joy occurs in heaven when what was lost is restored to its proper relationship with God. The joy we experience at reunions is a living metaphor; it reminds us of the joy in God's presence when our relationship with him is restored to its original design.

An artist friend told me that portraying shining light in a picture is very difficult. The artist accomplishes this feat by surrounding the light area with dark shapes. In the same way, we see the brilliance of joy at a reunion only when it is contrasted with the dark pain of separation. Joy occurs in heaven when a sinner repents. The dark pain, which both God and the person who was lost experienced, is gone, and the proper relationship of a person with God has been restored.

Another experience sometimes used to illustrate joy is when a team wins the championship at an athletic event. If you saw the film *Invictus*, what emotions did you feel when, at the end of the movie, the South African team defeated the greatly favored team from New Zealand? In situations like this, the emotions we feel are complex. We experience a combination of excitement, enthusiasm, and happiness. We commonly call this mixture of emotions "joy."

We find biblical examples of this kind of joy. Jews experience joy at Passover, a feast celebrating their deliverance from slavery in Egypt. This deliverance involved God's triumph over the Egyptians, who all drowned in the Red Sea.

Christians celebrate Easter with joy. Easter celebrates Jesus's triumph over death. In John 16:20–22, Jesus said, "Truly, truly, I say to you, that you will weep and lament, but the world will rejoice; you will grieve, but your grief will be turned into joy. Whenever a woman is in labor she has pain, because her hour has come; but when she gives birth to the child, she no longer remembers the anguish because of the joy that a child has been born into the world. Therefore you too have grief now; but I will see you again and your heart will rejoice, and no one will take your joy away from you." Jesus was talking to his disciples, who would grieve when he was taken from them and crucified. But they would rejoice when his resurrection reunited them. As Christians we believe that Jesus rose from the dead. That belief can be a root of joy even in the midst of suffering and pain.

The joy experienced after an athletic triumph is intensified when difficulties have been overcome for the triumph to occur. In the film *Invictus*, the South African team had to overcome many difficulties and master the skills needed to play rugby against a superior opponent. We experience enhanced joy when we have had to master skills and overcome difficulties to reach a goal. The Italians have a special word for this kind of joy: *fiero*. [1]

Joy: The Insight of Others

Because the experience of joy is so fundamental, it is difficult to define. For fundamental experiential things like joy, glory, and love, the best we can do is use words that describe our experiences. For joy, some of these words are *gladness, happiness, satisfaction, delight,* and *excitement*. Dallas Willard tries to define joy when he says, "Joy is a pervasive sense…of overall and ultimate well-being with a primary feeling component of delight." [2] Louis Smedes calls joy "the ecstasy of gratitude" and adds that we experience joy when our hearts are filled with gratefulness for some gifts, especially gifts of grace. [3] In one of John Piper's sermons about joy, he says, "Christian joy is not an act of willpower. It is a spontaneous emotional response of the heart."[4]

Think of your own life. When has joy come to you? Sometimes it comes when something good happens unexpectedly. Sometimes it comes when something bad suddenly turns good. St. Teresa of Avila talked about it coming unexpectedly in the midst of meditation and contemplation.[5] She used the Spanish word *gusto* to describe the experience. Louis Smedes agrees with John Piper and reminds us that we cannot do anything to make joy happen but that we *can* do things that *hinder* joy from coming. He talks about our need to recognize and free ourselves from attachments in our lives that keep joy away. He lists some of the myths we hang onto that prevent us from experiencing joy. [6] Two steps we can take to prepare ourselves to receive joy are cultivating gratitude and practicing intimacy with Jesus. These steps provide the soil out of which joy may spring, but we cannot bring joy through willpower.

The Roots of Joy

In his book *Living with Men*, E. James Wilder argues that God has designed our brains so we seek joy from the very beginning of our lives. [7] Every baby's brain is wired to seek joy from his or her caregivers from the moment the baby is born. The infant experiences this joy first by nourishment, warmth, and touch; then by eye contact and smiles; and later by words and sounds. This joy is relational in nature. The caregiver senses this joy and reflects it in his or her face and in other nonverbal ways. As discussed in a previous chapter, the infant copies these nonverbal expressions of joy and shares the emotion. This sharing of joy becomes like a dance the infant and caregiver experience as the infant grows.[8] In this dance the baby's brain is stimulated to grow and establish a unique and stable identity. This part of the brain never stops developing, so we adults still experience joy when we interact with others, with whom we can share our hearts. They then look at us with delight in their eyes, smile at us, and touch us appropriately.

I encourage you to do the project described below so you can share in a practical experience of this joy-sharing phenomenon.

A PROJECT FOR EXPLORING A JOY EXPERIENCE

1. Make arrangements to get together with a friend.
2. Before you meet, each of you should write a paragraph on a piece of paper. (If you desire, you may do this when you meet.)
3. Begin your paragraph with the words, "I am a person who…" Then continue your paragraph with the following:
4. "Thinks about (or believes)…" (List two or three things you think about.)
5. "Feels…when…" (List two or three feelings and the circumstances when these feelings show up.)
6. "Desires (or likes to)…" (Share some desires from your life.)
7. "Dreams about…" (What is one of your dreams for your life?)
8. Find a comfortable place where you and your friend can face each other. Each of you should read your paragraph to the other person. Then let the conversation go where it pleases for the next ten minutes or so.

What kind of emotions did you experience as each of you shared your paragraph? How would you describe this experience?

Dr. Wilder uses two metaphors when talking about the development of our joy-experiencing capacity. One metaphor, mentioned in Chapter 3, is "joy camp"; the second metaphor is "climbing joy mountain." An infant climbs joy mountain when there is an ongoing interaction with the caregiver that increases the intensity of the pleasure he or she experiences.[9] For example, young children climb joy mountain when they want to swing and ask the caregiver to push them so they can go higher and higher.

Adult Christians sometimes climb joy mountain when they worship. I can remember worship times when I had a growing experience of the glory of God mixed with the experience of his acceptance and love for me. As this experience grew in intensity, tingles ran up and down my spine. I had just experienced "climbing joy mountain." It is right that these worship experiences lead to intense joy because we will later discover that God is at the top of joy mountain. I only wish these experiences were more frequent.

Joy camp is the place of contentment, satisfaction, and happiness—when things are well with us. One can tell when a baby is at joy camp; the infant smiles, makes joyful sounds, and wiggles his or her arms and legs in happiness. A toddler is at joy camp when he or she successfully learns to walk or gets a toy he or she wants. A young boy is at joy camp when he rides his bicycle and feels the wind brush his face and hair.

One task of caregivers is to help infants spend as much time at joy camp as possible. Life, however, doesn't allow us to spend all our time at joy camp. One cannot live very long without experiencing a trauma, a hard thing. Because we live in a sinful world, many infants and young people have had very little experience at joy camp. So a second task of caregivers is to model returning to joy camp after someone has experienced a "hard thing," which is anything that takes away our joy. (Do you remember the illustration we gave of this in Chapter 3?)

The example of joy camp Dr. Wilder mentions in his book is taking a group of young people backpacking in the mountains. It was a difficult climb, and at one time the group got lost and had to look for the trail. They experienced discouragement and a lot of "hard things." Finally, at the end they reached a lovely campsite, unloaded their packs, fixed a meal, and enjoyed a relaxing and beautiful evening. They experienced coming back to joy camp after struggling through many hard things.

In the Bible, joy is related to the Hebrew word *shalom*. This word, usually translated "peace," has a larger meaning that involves a sense of well-being along with delight that everything is as God intended it to be. I believe that returning to joy camp after experiencing difficulties is coming into shalom. Can you feel this if you imagine yourself in the shoes of the back-packers in Dr. Wilder's example?

A Key Development Task

These stories bring us to the discussion of the key developmental task mentioned in Chapter 3. This task is to learn how to return to joy after experiencing trauma in our lives. Negative emotions accompany these traumas. The emotions we have discussed so far in this book—shame, fear, anger, and sadness—are examples. Our challenge as adults is to learn how to return to joy camp when we experience these emotions. Many of us may not have had much experience in accomplishing this task during our developmental years, so we must learn to do it now—and that is often difficult.

In Chapter 1, we introduced the story of Jesus teaching in the synagogue at Nazareth. We concluded that Jesus came into the world to bring release and freedom to those who were oppressed or imprisoned. Using the metaphors in this chapter, we see that one way of rephrasing this purpose is to say that Jesus came to bring those who have been traumatized back into joy camp. The gospel is "good news" because God desires to bring back into joy those who have been oppressed by traumas in their lives.

Providing the opportunity for Jesus to do this is the outcome we seek when we learn to converse with him about our negative emotions. During these conversations we experience intimacy with Jesus. We will see below that joy is a prime characteristic of the nature of God. So when we experience intimacy with Jesus, he is able to bring joy back into our lives. In the synagogue at Nazareth, Jesus quoted from Isaiah 61:1–2. Continuing in verse 3, this passage describes what the return to joy camp looks like. Isaiah said that the Messiah will give "them a garland instead of ashes, the oil of gladness instead of mourning, the mantle of praise instead of a spirit of fainting."

In the passage quoted at the beginning of this chapter, the prophet Isaiah also gave a prophetic picture of what Jesus accomplishes for his people. "And the ransomed of the Lord will return and come with joyful shouting to Zion, with everlasting joy upon their heads. They will find gladness and joy, and sorrow and sighing will flee away" (Isa. 35:10).

As we go through the Scriptures, we find that joy is a central characteristic of the nature of the triune God. "In Your presence is fullness of joy; in Your right hand there are pleasures forever" (Ps. 16:11). Joy comes with the experience of the presence of God. Jesus said in John 15:11, "These things I have spoken to you so that My joy may be in you, and that your joy may be made full." What things had he been speaking about? He'd been talking about abiding in the vine and saying that he was the vine.

When we experience abiding in Jesus, God enables us to experience joy, because joy is an essential part of the nature of the Trinity. We see a picture of how the expectation of joy in the presence of God can help us endure traumatic events, especially when we meditate on Hebrews 12:2. "Fixing our eyes on Jesus, the author and perfecter of faith, who for the joy set before Him endured the cross, despising the shame, and has sat down at the right hand of the throne of God." I believe this verse gives us a picture of the greatest cosmic trauma.

Jesus experienced unimaginable torture and shame, but he was able to endure the torture and despise the shame because he could see himself returning to the right hand of God, where, as Psalm 16:11 reminds us, we find "fullness of joy; in Your right hand there are pleasures forever." Jesus can function as our Great High Priest because he knows how to join us in our pain and trauma, and help us endure the trauma and despise the shame we feel. He does this by reminding us of the joy that exists in his presence.

To be in the presence of God is to be enraptured with joy. Do you think Jesus, the Father, and the Holy Spirit experienced *fiero* when Jesus triumphed over death and broke the power of sin to dominate our lives? And as he now exists at the Father's right hand, interceding for us? (Heb. 7:25).

The psalmist had a revelation of how God's presence brought joy to all around him when he said that the mountains and trees would sing and the rivers would clap their hands for joy when they contemplate the coming of the Lord (Ps. 96:12; 98:8). Even nature has to rejoice when God manifests his presence.

In both the Old and New Testaments, God commands joy. "Delight yourself in the Lord; and He will give you the desires of your heart" (Ps. 37:4). "Shout joyfully to the Lord, all the earth. Serve the Lord with gladness; come before Him with joyful singing" (Ps. 100:1–2). "Rejoice in the Lord always; again I will say, rejoice!" (Phil. 4:4). "Rejoice always" (1 Thess. 5:16).

When we were listing the efforts of various people to define joy, both John Piper and Lewis Smedes agreed that "Christian joy is not an act of willpower. It is a spontaneous emotional response of the heart."[10] Our dilemma is this: if joy is not an act of human willpower, how can God command us to be joyful? We are faced with a situation where God seemingly asks us to do something beyond our capacity. This should not surprise us, because God is always asking people to do things beyond their ability.

For example, when God called Moses to deliver his people from Egypt, Moses became intensely aware of his inability to do so (you can read the story in Exodus 3–4). A similar situation arose when God called Gideon to deliver his people from the Midianites (see Judg. 6–7). In both situations, the way out of the dilemma was that God promised to be present with them. It was not human will or strength that enabled these men to do what God had asked; it was the promise that God would be present and accomplish his work. So I believe this is the way out of our dilemma about being joyful when we, in our own strength, cannot be joyful using our willpower. The presence of God gives us the ability to obey his commands.

The Scriptures tell us that joy is a fruit of the Spirit (Gal. 5:22). As we learn more about how to abide in Jesus, his joy comes to us as a supernatural gift. God provides the Holy Spirit to give us the capacity to obey his command to rejoice. Our part is to learn to abide in Jesus and cultivate the soil of our hearts so joy can come forth. When we experience the presence of Jesus, we open ourselves to experience all the fruit of the Spirit. Louis Smedes pointed out that our attachments to other things can hinder our ability to experience the presence of Jesus, so another way for us to do "our part" is to seek revelation from God about our attachments to other things that hinder abiding in him.

Earlier in this chapter, we talked about situations that stimulate joy. The first of these was a reunion. We gave scriptural examples of things that were lost but later found. We pointed out that a necessary precursor to experiencing this kind of joy is the pain we feel during separation and loss. We experience joy when this pain is removed due to the return of the loved one to the place where he or she belongs. The Scriptures clearly distinguish Christian joy from our common use of the word *happiness* by emphasizing that we can experience Christian joy in the presence of painful trauma.

To illustrate this truth, let's look at Romans 5:1–5. "Therefore, having been justified by faith, we have peace with God through our Lord Jesus Christ, through whom also we have obtained our introduction by faith into this grace in which we stand; and we exult in hope of the glory of God. And not only this, but we also exult in our tribulations, knowing that tribulation brings about perseverance; and perseverance, proven character; and proven character, hope; and hope does not disappoint, because the love of God has been poured out within our hearts through the Holy Spirit who was given to us."

The word *exult* means "to feel extreme happiness and elation" and "to express great joy." The passage tells us we should experience this feeling and manifest this expression in the midst of tribulation. *Tribulation* is an older word we don't use very much in present English. Today we would use words like *trouble, pain, trauma,* or *difficulty.* James 1:2–4 gives us an identical message. "Consider it all joy, my brethren, when you encounter various trials, knowing that the testing of your faith produces endurance. And let endurance have its perfect result, so that you may be perfect and complete, lacking in nothing." In both of these passages, trials are linked with endurance, and endurance produces growth. Experiencing and expressing joy in the midst of painful circumstances lead to hope and to experiencing the love of God more deeply.

We now have a second dilemma surrounding joy. This dilemma brings together many of the things we have discovered about Christian joy. We can see that the situation discussed in Romans 5:1–5 is about returning to joy camp in the midst of, or following, a trauma. All tribulation and suffering are traumas. Our challenge is to learn how to return to joy camp after such experiences.

Our return to joy camp is connected to hope in a God who is good and will one day make everything right. The Scriptures emphasize this theme. "For momentary, light affliction is producing for us an eternal weight of glory far beyond all comparison" (2 Cor. 4:17). "The sufferings of this present time are not worthy to be compared with the glory that is to be revealed to us" (Rom. 8:18).

The model conversations with God about the negative emotions we experience are practical tools for us to experience God's love and care for us when we are in the midst of painful feelings. Ideally, as we have these conversations with him, we can see the light in his face and the delight in his eyes as he identifies with our pain, takes us by the hand, and gives us a new vision of his love and care for us. When we can sense this, we are on our way back to joy camp.

I believe this experience is what a famous Old Testament benediction aims for. "The Lord bless you, and keep you; the Lord make His face shine on you, and be gracious to you; the Lord lift up His countenance on you, and give you peace" (Num. 6:24–26). Remember that we experience joy as we look in the face of someone who loves us, and that joy and shalom (peace) are closely connected. The Lord, our loving caregiver, can bring us back to joy camp.

Our passage, Romans 5:1–5, reminds us that as we participate in this process of letting Jesus bring us back to joy by inspiring hope, the Holy Spirit, whom God has given to us, pours God's love into our hearts.

Some of us may have had past experiences that erect huge barriers to seeing God as looking at us with delight. What do we do if this is the case? My suggestion is to go back to the message of the gospel and the historical fact of the cross, and ask the Holy Spirit to pour out the love of God within our hearts.

God really does love you. Do you believe that? One might respond, "Yes, I believe that with my mind. The rider believes that. But I don't think the elephant believes that." In this situation I believe we need a flesh-and-blood person to help us…a counselor, a mentor, a close and trusted friend. Someone who can help us train our elephants—someone who can help the elephants get us back to joy camp.

The previous chapters emphasized that Jesus is a real person who is alive; he can help us learn to lead the elephants back to joy camp so we can share the deep things of our hearts with him. But God's intention is also that we be part of a loving community, where we can find flesh-and-blood people who will help us believe that God loves us, that he delights in that we are in his family, and that we have a future and a hope. When we have a future and a hope, the fruit of joy appears in our lives, even in the midst of suffering and tribulation.

Our Conversation with Jesus about Joy

What we have learned about joy explains what we would like to happen in all our conversations with Jesus. One of the purposes of Jesus's life and sacrifice for us was to bring us back to joy from the many dark and traumatic places where we find ourselves in the midst of this life. These dark and traumatic places involve the negative emotions and the destructive actions and attitudes to which they move us.

We begin our conversation with Jesus about joy by establishing a relational connection with him. If you need to be refreshed in how to do this, go back to the discussions in Chapters 2 and 3 about practicing the presence of Jesus, our High Priest.

Your conversation with Jesus will be an individual experience that depends on your particular situation. I offer the following model conversation to give you a place where you might start to develop this spiritual discipline.

> Jesus, I thank you that you desire to be with me, to join me in all of my emotions and thoughts. The Scriptures tell me that you delight to be with me. Sometimes it is hard for me to experience your presence in my heart. Help me to look into your face and see the sparkle in your eyes as you anticipate having this conversation with me.

> Jesus, you promised to be with me until the end of the age. I thank you that you are with me now as I experience this dark place in

my life. I want to get back to joy camp, but I can't do it by myself. Thank you that you want to join me and help me carry the pain I'm experiencing. And I thank you that you want to give me a vision of what it will be like when I can experience your presence more fully. When that happens, help me to have a glimpse of the joy and pleasure that will be in your presence. Scripture tells me that what I am experiencing now in my life is just a momentary, light affliction, not worthy to be compared with the glory that will be revealed. Help me, Jesus, to look at the things that are unseen, the eternal, rather than at the things that are seen, the temporal.

Jesus, help me to learn to abide in you. I want your joy to be part of my everyday life. You have promised that if I abide in you, your joy would be in me and that my joy would be full. This is the kind of life I would like to learn to live, a life that can rejoice in trouble because I know you will pour your love into my heart and strengthen my hope of sharing your glory in my future life with you. Help me to experience a life in which Isaiah 61:10 becomes the foundation of my life. "I will rejoice greatly in the Lord, my soul will exult in my God; for He has clothed me with garments of salvation, He has wrapped me with a robe of righteousness, as a bridegroom decks himself with a garland, and as a bride adorns herself with her jewels."

CONCLUSION

My prayer is that all who read this book will no longer want to deny their emotions or be afraid of them. Rather, I pray that you would see your emotions as a path to deeper intimacy with the triune God, who has done everything possible to bring us into his family. He invites us to share in the dance of joy that will continue throughout eternity in his presence. Will you respond to his invitation?

ENDNOTES

CHAPTER 2

1. I am indebted to Professor Jonathan Haidt, who introduced me to this metaphor and discusses the difficulties we have with internal conflicts. Jonathan Haidt, *The Happiness Hypothesis* (New York: Basic Books, 2006), 1–22.

2. Paul Sherman, "Elephant with Rider," Wpclipart.com, accessed December 10, 2012, http://www.wpclipart.com/animals/E/elephant/elephant_2/elephant_with_rider.png.html.

3. Tom Marshall, *Living in the Freedom of the Spirit* (Tonbridge, Kent: Sovereign World Ltd., 2001), 51–81.

4. Antonio Damasio, *Descartes' Error: Emotion, Reason, and the Human Brain* (New York: Putnam, 1994). 3–19, 34–51.

5. Daniel J. Siegel, *The Developing Mind* (New York: Guilford Press, 1999), 245.

6. Karl Lehman, "Brain Science, Psychological Trauma, and the God Who Is with Us, Part II: The Processing Pathway for Painful Experiences and the Definition of Psychological Trauma," Kclehman.com, last modified February 4, 2011, http://www.kclehman.com/download.php?doc=131.

7. E. James Wilder, "Neurotheology on Emotion," The Life Model, accessed September 10, 2007, http://www.lifemodel.org/wordhtml/neuroth_03.htm.

8. Dan B. Allender and Tremper Longman III, *The Cry of the Soul* (Colorado Springs, CO: NavPress, 1994), 14. Doctors Allender and Longman argue with the idea that emotions are amoral. They correctly state that our fallenness has affected our emotions. My point is that the core feeling needs to be accepted and acknowledged before we make moral judgments about it. I believe the authors would agree with the end result of my argument.

9. The emphasis of this book is learning how to converse with Jesus about our emotions, but also important is developing relationships with safe people, with whom we can talk about our emotions.

CHAPTER 3

1. I have borrowed the terms "joy center" and "joy camp" from Dr. James Wilder. E. James Wilder, *The Complete Guide to Living with Men* (Pasadena, CA: Shepherd's House, 2004), 13.
2. Lehman, "Brain Science," 14–15.
3. John Bradshaw, *Healing the Shame That Binds You* (Deerfield Beach, FL: Health Communications, 2005), 5, 21.
4. Lewis B. Smedes, *Shame and Grace* (New York: HarperCollins, 1993), 31–44.
5. Frank B. Minirth and Paul D. Meier, *Counseling and the Nature of Man* (Grand Rapids, MI: Baker, 1982), 29-35. This section presents an overview of defense mechanisms. Denial is the first one mentioned in the list of specific defense mechanisms on p. 35.
6. Smedes, *Shame and Grace*, 108.
7. Leanne Payne, *Restoring the Christian Soul through Healing Prayer* (Wheaton, IL: Crossway Books, 1991), 67–102. This book gives an excellent discussion of how receiving forgiveness for our sins and releasing forgiveness to others can free us into our new identity.
8. E. James Wilder and Chris M. Coursey, *Share Immanuel: The Healing Lifestyle* (Pasadena, CA: Shepherd's House, 2010), 4–6. The procedure I use is a modification of the practice described in this book.
9. Ibid., 3–4. The author pictures our pain memories as fiery thorn bushes at the bottom of a hill. The two seats where we experience the presence of God are at the top of the hill. In my presentation, shame feelings correspond to the thorn bushes.
10. Ibid., 10–13.

CHAPTER 4

1. Jerry Seinfeld, quoted in Sora Song, "Health: The Price of Pressure," *Time,* July 19, 2004.

2. For an excellent discussion of the destructive effects of too much excitement, see Archibald Hart, *Thrilled to Death* (Nashville: Thomas Nelson, 2007), 57–72.

3. Archibald Hart, *The Anxiety Cure* (Nashville: Thomas Nelson, 1999), 26. I recommend this book for an overview of anxiety disorders and ways to treat all forms of anxiety.

4. Herbert Benson and Marg Stark, *Timeless Healing* (New York: Fireside, 1996), 123–148.

5. Lehman, "Brain Science," 13–14.

6. John Piper, *The Pleasures of God* (Sisters, OR: Multnomah, 2000), 197–199. This book is a series of meditations on Scripture passages that talk about what gives God pleasure. I highly recommend it for your devotional reading.

7. Hart, *Anxiety Cure*, 153–167. The author gives detailed ideas for disciplines that will free us from the destructive effects of worry anxiety.

CHAPTER 5

1. Dennis L. Okholm, "To Vent or Not to Vent? What Contemporary Psychology Can Learn from Ascetic Theology about Anger," quoted in Mark R. McMinn and Timothy R. Phillips, eds., *Care for the Soul* (Downers Grove, IL: InterVarsity, 2001), 186.

2. Solomon Schimmel, *The Seven Deadly Sins: Jewish, Christian, and Classical Reflections on Human Psychology* (New York: Free Press, 1992), 83.

3. Allender and Longman, *Cry of the Soul*, 58.

4. Ibid., 55–77. The authors devote two chapters to distinguishing between unrighteous and righteous anger.

5. Adapted from a lecture Dr. William Backus gave in a counseling course at the University of the Nations (Kona, Hawaii) campus in 1996. See William Backus for his recommendations for treating anger. William Backus, *Telling the Truth to Troubled People* (Minneapolis: Bethany House, 1985), 156–170.

6. Neil Clark Warren, "Anger Management," *Counsel Tapes*, The American Association of Christian Counselors, 2001. I have

constructed Figure 5-2 using some material from this taped lecture.

7.   Stephen R. Covey, *The 7 Habits of Highly Effective People* (New York: Simon & Schuster, 1989), 235–260.

8.   Les Carter and Frank Minirth, *The Anger Workbook* (Nashville: Thomas Nelson, 1993), 8–19.

9.   Allender and Longman, *Cry of the Soul*, 58, 66–68.

10. A Christian brother or sister who has experienced the practice of "two or three agreeing" can help us in this part of our conversation with God. See Matt. 18:19–20. Also see Payne, *Restoring the Christian Soul*, 153–155.

11. Allender and Longman, *Cry of the Soul*, 65–66.

12. Lehman, "Brain Science," 12.

CHAPTER 6

1.   Archibald D. Hart, *Unmasking Male Depression* (Nashville: Thomas Nelson, 2001), 69–73. Dr. Hart's point is that cybersex is one of the ways we seek to medicate the pain of our losses.

2.   Alan Chapman, "Elisabeth Kübler-Ross—Five Stages of Grief," Businessballs.com, accessed December 19, 2012, http://www.businessballs.com/elisabeth_kubler_ross_five_stages_of_grief.htm. For more information, please see Elizabeth Kubler-Ross, *On Grief and Grieving: Finding the Meaning of Grief through the Five Stages of Loss* (New York: Simon & Schuster, 2005).

3.   George E. Vaillant, *Spiritual Evolution: A Scientific Defense of Faith* (New York: Broadway Books, 2008), 102–118.

4.   David G. Benner, *Sacred Companions: The Gift of Spiritual Friendship and Direction* (Downers Grove, IL: InterVarsity, 2002), 61–81.

5.   For an excellent treatment of reactive depression, see Archibald D. Hart, *Counseling the Depressed* (Dallas: Word, 1987), 73–86. Dr. Hart includes a biblical perspective on loss.

6.   Hart, *Unmasking Male Depression*, 64–66.

7.   James G. Friesen, et al., *Living from the Heart Jesus Gave You* (Pasadena, CA: Shepherd's House, 2000), 42–55. This section

describes Type A and B traumas and ways to bring healing into them.

8. Robert Karen, *The Forgiving Self* (New York: Doubleday, 2001), 49–50.

9. Martin Seligman, *Authentic Happiness* (New York: Free Press, 2002), 75–81.

CHAPTER 7

1. Paul Ekman, *Emotions Revealed* (New York: Henry Holt, 2003), 196–197.

2. Dallas Willard, *Renovation of the Heart* (Colorado Springs, CO: NavPress, 2002), 132.

3. Smedes, *Shame and Grace*, 159.

4. John Piper, "Christian Joy, the Fruit of Hope," radio broadcast, Desiring God Radio, February 24, 2005.

5. Gerald G. May, *The Dark Night of the Soul* (New York: Harper-Collins, 2004), 103–134.

6. Smedes, *Shame and Grace*, 161–164.

7. Wilder, *Living with Men*, 13–18.

8. There is a wonderful description of this dance in David Brooks, *The Social Animal* (New York: Random House, 2011), 36–49.

9. God has built in a safety valve for us when we climb joy mountain. When the stimulation gets too intense, the infant signals by looking away. Wilder, *Living with Men,* 19. This signal means a calming time is needed. Having a repeated experience of climbing joy mountain, followed by calming, teaches us how to be stimulated to joy and then how to calm ourselves. When we forget our need to have a calming time, we may fall into anhedonia, the inability to experience pleasure. Hart, *Thrilled to Death*, 57–69.

10. John Piper, "Christian Joy." Smedes, *Shame and Grace,* 161.

Bibliography

Allender, Dan B., and Tremper Longman III. *The Cry of the Soul.* Colorado Springs, CO: NavPress, 1994.

Backus, William. *Telling the Truth to Troubled People.* Minneapolis: Bethany House, 1985.

Benner, David G. *Sacred Companions: The Gift of Spiritual Friendship and Direction.* Downers Grove, IL: InterVarsity, 2002.

Benson, Herbert, and Marg Stark. *Timeless Healing.* New York: Fireside, 1996.

Bradshaw, John. *Healing the Shame That Binds You.* Deerfield Beach, FL: Health Communications, 2005.

Brooks, David. *The Social Animal.* New York: Random House, 2011.

Carter, Les, and Frank Minirth. *The Anger Workbook.* Nashville: Thomas Nelson, 1993.

Covey, Stephen R. *The 7 Habits of Highly Effective People.* New York: Simon & Schuster, 1989.

Damasio, Antonio. *Descartes' Error: Emotion, Reason, and the Human Brain.* New York: Putnam, 1994.

Ekman, Paul. *Emotions Revealed.* New York: Henry Holt, 2003.

Friesen, James G., E. James Wilder, Anne M. Bierling, Rick Koepcke, and Maribeth Poole. *Living from the Heart Jesus Gave You.* Pasadena, CA: Shepherd's House, 2000.

Haidt, Jonathan. *The Happiness Hypothesis.* New York: Basic Books, 2006.

Hart, Archibald. *The Anxiety Cure.* Nashville: Thomas Nelson, 1999.

Hart, Archibald. *Counseling the Depressed.* Dallas: Word, 1987.

Hart, Archibald. *Thrilled to Death.* Nashville: Thomas Nelson, 2007.

Hart, Archibald. *Unmasking Male Depression.* Nashville: Thomas Nelson, 2001.

Karen, Robert. *The Forgiving Self.* New York: Doubleday, 2001.

Kubler-Ross, Elizabeth. *On Grief and Grieving: Finding the Meaning of Grief through the Five Stages of Loss.* New York: Simon & Schuster, 2005.

Marshall, Tom. *Living in the Freedom of the Spirit.* Tonbridge, Kent: Sovereign World Ltd., 2001.

May, Gerald G. *The Dark Night of the Soul.* New York: HarperCollins, 2004.

Minirth, Frank B, and Paul D. Meier. *Counseling and the Nature of Man.* Grand Rapids, MI: Baker, 1982.

Okholm, Dennis L. "To Vent or Not to Vent? What Contemporary Psychology Can Learn from Ascetic Theology about Anger." In McMinn, Mark R., and Timothy R. Phillips, eds. *Care for the Soul.* Downers Grove, IL: InterVarsity, 2001.

Payne, Leanne. *Restoring the Christian Soul through Healing Prayer.* Wheaton, IL: Crossway Books, 1991.

Piper, John. *The Pleasures of God.* Sisters, OR: Multnomah, 2000.

Piper, John. "Christian Joy, the Fruit of Hope." Radio broadcast. Minneapolis: Desiring God Radio, February 24, 2005.

Schimmel, Solomon. *The Seven Deadly Sins: Jewish, Christian, and Classical Reflections on Human Psychology.* New York: Free Press, 1992.

Seligman, Martin. *Authentic Happiness.* New York: Free Press, 2002.

Siegel, Daniel J. *The Developing Mind.* New York: Guilford Press, 1999.

Smedes, Lewis B. *Shame and Grace.* New York: HarperCollins, 1993.

Song, Sora. "Health: The Price of Pressure." *Time,* July 19, 2004.

Vaillant, George E. *Spiritual Evolution: A Scientific Defense of Faith.* New York: Broadway Books, 2008.

Warren, Neil Clark. "Anger Management." *Counsel Tapes.* Forest, VA: The American Association of Christian Counselors, 2001.

Wilder, E. James. *The Complete Guide to Living with Men.* Pasadena, CA: Shepherd's House, 2004.

Wilder, E. James, and Chris M. Coursey. *Share Immanuel: The Healing Lifestyle.* Pasadena, CA: Shepherd's House, 2010.

Willard, Dallas. *Renovation of the Heart.* Colorado Springs, CO: NavPress, 2002.

Connect with the author

E-mail: mel@moodfoodbook.com

Website: www.moodfoodbook.com